HEALTH CARE 2020

THE COMING COLLAPSE OF EMPLOYER-PROVIDED HEALTH CARE

HEALTH CARE 2020

THE COMING COLLAPSE OF EMPLOYER-PROVIDED HEALTH CARE

WILLIAM STYRING III
AND
DONALD K. JONAS

HUDSON INSTITUTE
INDIANAPOLIS, INDIANA

362.10973
593h

Hudson Institute
Indianapolis, Indiana

$16.95
ISBN #1-55813-066-7
Copyright© 1999 Hudson Institute, Inc.
All rights reserved. No part of this publication may be reproduced, by any process or technique, without the express written consent of the publisher, except in the case of brief quotations embodied in critical articles and reviews.

The views of this book are solely the views of the authors. No opinions, statement of fact, or conclusions contained in this document can be properly attributed to Hudson Institute, its staff, its members, or its contracting agencies.

Printed in the United States of America

This book may be ordered from:
Hudson Institute
Herman Kahn Center
P.O. Box 26-919
Indianapolis, Indiana 46226
(317) 545-1000
1-800-HUDSON-Ø

TABLE OF CONTENTS

University Libraries
Carnegie Mellon University
Pittsburgh, PA 15213-3890

LIST OF ILLUSTRATIONS

Charts

Tables

PREFACE

This book continues a long tradition for the Hudson Institute—that of taking the long view, of considering where our society is headed, of "futurism." Through that tradition, we have benefited from the Institute's analyses. Today, we are confronting a crucial public policy question, and the Hudson Institute once again is stoking the fires of an important public discussion.

Institute researchers have been writing about the implications of the aging of Baby Boomers for fifteen years. The Boomers, born between 1946 and 1964, constitute the largest generation in American history. As we move past the threshold of the year 2000 they will be in their mid-50s; they will begin retiring in the first decade of the third millennium, and by the year 2020, many of the 76 million Baby Boomers will be over 70 years of age—and requiring more extensive health care.

This book considers the fundamental issue of how the aging Baby Boomers will affect the financing and delivery of health care, not only their own, but that of younger generations as well. How will the much smaller "Baby Bust" generation which follows deal with the health care demands of the Boomer generation? How will they finance their own health care?

Health care delivery is among the most important questions Americans will face in the early decades of the next century. As anyone involved in health care knows, this field is undergoing a terrific sea change that has begun well in advance of the Baby Boomers' aging, and it must be resolved if we are to successfully pass through the increase in clinical activity they are likely to produce. Continued medical advances are the best answer to the public's need—and plea—for the best medical care. Indeed, the very success of medical discovery, which offers options to virtually all individuals facing major health problems, has been the single major contributor to the current concern about health policy. Yet in this circumstance nothing is more key, now and into the future, than the continued advancement of academic medicine—medical (and public health) research, education, and clinical care. These are crucial to our ability to provide appropriate care to individuals of every age, and to reflect clearly on the best and most balanced handling of these important issues.

Regardless of one's views on the complicated, and sometimes controversial, topic of health care delivery into the next century, it is most important that the matter be brought into serious public discussion. The Hudson Institute's willingness to do so in a detailed and lively manner is a service to us all.

Bernadine P. Healy, M.D.
Dean, College of Medicine and Public Health
The Ohio State University
The Cleveland Clinic Foundation

ACKNOWLEDGEMENTS
AND
AN INTRODUCTION TO HEALTH CARE 2020

This is a book about what the health care system might look like in the year 2020.

It is not a book about what medical technology will be like in the year 2020. The authors are an economist and a political scientist respectively, and have no special expertise in medical research. Even if we were molecular biologists, it is not likely that any predictions we might make about medicine per se in the year 2020 would be given much weight.

The year 2020 is twenty-one years down the road. Will we have a cure for cancer? Recent press reports indicate that studies of mice injected with experimental drugs show promise of starving tumors of new blood supplies, thereby curing the underlying cancers. One fervently hopes that is the case, but the history of cancer research has been that of producing therapies in rodents that have not worked in humans.

What about cures for the common cold by the year 2020? The common cold is caused by the almost infinitely mutatable rhinovirus. We do not know, nor does anyone, whether there is a therapy on the horizon that offers a cure for our annual winter sneezes.

Nor can anyone be certain about how medical devices and drugs will evolve by the year 2020.

To test this assertion, consider going back twenty-one years to 1978. What could have been predicted in 1978 about medical technology in 1999? Probably not a great deal.

In 1975, one of the authors sired a baby boy. The labor was long and hard. The mother, the wife of the coauthor, was in agony. Four years later, with the birth of the second child, anesthesiology had produced the epidural—the

"Cadillac" childbirth painkiller—and the birth was nearly pain-free. Perhaps those in the know would have been privy to this future development, but an economist-father certainly was not.

In 1978, the term "gene-splicing" or "biotechnology" would have provoked a dumbfounded gaze. Now we have a major "big science" effort to unravel the entire human genome. Perhaps this project will succeed in the early or mid part of the first decade of the next century. Maybe it will not. If it does, astonishing therapies may become commonplace in the year 2020. No one knows just what they will be, or if they will be. Or if success will drive down medical costs by rendering currently expensive therapies obsolete, or drive them up by making the currently untreatable susceptible to medical intervention.

In 1978, would anyone have guessed about the progress in neonatal care, enabling ever-more premature babies to be saved?

Plausible speculations are endless. Perhaps by the year 2020 the cumbersome FDA drug approval and review process will so slow the introduction of new antibiotics that drug-resistant microbes will gain the upper hand, and we will all die from moderate ear infections! Analysts of the state of medicine today complain of a dearth of new antibiotics in the pipeline, and doctors reserve the one remaining "silver bullet" antibiotic, vancomycin, for last-ditch use for fear of creating a race of superbugs resistant to it.

The point is that while speculation about medical technology twenty-one years hence would be a great deal of fun, it would also not be a particularly illuminating exercise. Some of the guesses might turn out to be accurate— from luck. But it is almost certain that most of the speculations about medicine per se that we will see delivered in the year 2020 will be either partly off the mark or just dead wrong.

We therefore avoid such speculation as much as possible.

Instead, *Health Care 2020* is a book about how social, political, and especially demographic trends will affect the financing and methods of organization of the health care delivery system. Many of these sociopolitical and demographic trends can be projected out two decades with a high degree of certainty.

The tidal wave of 76 million Baby Boomers first reaching age 65 in the year 2011 is our prime example. This graying of America is a virtual certainty (unless a new, selective microbe which kills only the elderly should come along!). This is not "new news." Politicians, for example, are beginning to bestir themselves over the bleak prospects for Social Security when all of those Boomers demand what they have been promised from the government retirement system.

While the coming increase in the number of older Americans relative to younger Americans may not come as news to those who have been paying attention, we contend that far from all of the implications for health care of this demographic implosion have been thought through.

Medicare, of course, will be a greatly shrunken version of what it is today. The bioethics debate in the year 2020—e.g., how many quadruple bypasses can we afford for 85-year-olds, and who will pay for them if they are to be paid for at all?—will be a much hotter discussion. There are even less obvious implications. We contend, for example, in Chapter 2 that the attempts by the Boomers to retire will forever change the present system of predominantly employment-based health insurance. To be replaced by—what? Single-payer government health insurance? Medical Savings Accounts? Some kind of tax credit for private health insurance purchase?

By the year 2020, the aging Baby Boomers will have severe health care implications for government, business, and every average American. It is best that we start thinking about them now.

This is a book written principally for the interested lay person and policymaker. We avoid jargon. We avoid endless academic citations, although our data are amply documented. We hope this is a readable book that tells a wide spectrum of American society how our health care system got to where it is and where it is likely to go.

We thank the Robert Wood Johnson Foundation for its generous financial support while crafting this book. The Hudson Institute research librarians were, as always, outstanding in their efforts. Other staff at Hudson contributed through their constant encouragement and friendly critiques of earlier drafts of various chapters. In particular, we thank our Hudson colleagues Greg Brinker, Sam Karnick, Rebecca Arrick, Linda McDonald, Susan Protsman, Barbara Husk, Herbert London, Barbara Johnson, and Sergio Stojkovich. They bear no responsibility for any mistakes we have no doubt made in our analysis.

Others contributed as well. Particularly important for Chapter 4 were Dr. Eleanor Kinney, Director of the Center for Law and Medicine at Indiana-Purdue University at Indianapolis; Deputy Director Robert Hornyak of the Bureau of Aging and In-Home Services, State of Indiana; Jena Walls and Ali Khan of the Indiana State Budget Agency; and Dr. John Grew, Chief of Staff of the Indiana House Ways and Means Committee. They also bear no responsibility for any of our errors.

Above all, we thank our wives for putting up with us.

William Styring III and Donald K. Jonas
Indianapolis, Indiana
June 1999

4

CHAPTER 1
EXECUTIVE SUMMARY AND INTRODUCTION TO THE GRAYING BOOMERS

Introducing the Baby Boomers

Baby Boomers are those 76 million Americans born between 1946 and 1964. By a wide margin, they are the largest generation in American history. The primary cause of this demographic bulge was World War II.

Returning World War II servicemen started families later than they might otherwise have but soon made up for the interruption in their lives. Births soared. In 1945, there were about 2.8 million births in the U.S. In 1946, the first year of the "Baby Boom," that number jumped to 3.8 million. Births remained at around 4 million a year through 1964 before falling off dramatically into a "Baby Bust." By then, potential mothers and fathers from the World War II generation, having reached middle age, had exhausted their desire for—and often ability to have—children.

As this huge group of Boomers age, they will force drastic changes in all aspects of American life, including health care.

This is a book primarily about how the Boomers will impact the U.S. health care delivery system: how it is now financed and how different it might be in the future, how it is organized and how it might be organized, and how much health care will then be available. What will health care look like in the year 2020 as the Boomers drop their formidable aged and expensive demographic weight on the health care system? By 2020, half of the Baby Boomers will have reached age 65. By 2030, all of them will have.

The Pig Through a Python

The Baby Boomers have always had a compelling impact on society because of their sheer numbers, like a "pig moving through a python."

Primary and Secondary Education

In the 1950s, as the first Boomers began attending school, school districts across the country scrambled to find places for them. Some used temporary classrooms or even resorted to half-day school, effectively creating two "shifts" of students. Almost all districts instituted massive building programs, and Schools of Education began churning out vast numbers of new teachers to teach the Boomer kids. Many school districts are even today facing tough decisions over the disposition of school buildings once built to accommodate the Boomers.

Sputnik, the USSR first satellite launch in 1957, caused a wave of national panic. Were we in the U.S. producing as many scientists and engineers as the Russians? How could we be behind in the Space Race? What could we do to improve the education of our Boomer children? The result was the first federal subsidies of K-12 education, and early-years Boomers who remember John Glenn strapped into an Atlas rocket. The Right Stuff.

College Years

In the mid-1960s, the first Boomers reached college age, and their high-participation rate in higher education was a remarkable phenomenon. Prior to World War II, attendance at college was comparatively rare, limited to the sons (and sometimes daughters) of the very affluent. Few others attended. The Baby Boom generation made higher education increasingly a middle- and even working-class activity. (It is interesting, though not necessarily significant, that scores on the Scholastic Aptitude Test began declining in 1964 when the first Boomers began taking the exam.) Many of the Boomers' parents had taken advantage of the GI Bill to gain degrees. Consequently, there was an attitudinal breakthrough that said, "Yes, there is no reason why my child shouldn't also go to college." Postwar economic growth put college within the financial reach of more households.

Boomers created the salad days of growth for higher education. Along the way, they also controlled popular culture through the 1960s counterculture and anti-Vietnam War movement. (One does not today see campus protests each night on the evening news as happened during the 1960s.)

The Markets

Boomers are now aged from their mid-30s to early 50s. They are in or near their peak earning years, and are once again having a disproportionate say-so in how events unfold. The oldest Baby Boomers are entering a zone where they are at least beginning to *think* about their future retirement.

We need not look far for an example. Now armed with defined contribution (401-k) retirement plans and Individual Retirement Accounts, Boomers are pouring money into the equity markets at a breathtaking rate, driving stocks to levels thought impossible just a few years ago. The Dow Jones Industrial average was at 4000 as recently as 1994. Nearly 20 million Boomers own 401-k plans, with assets approaching $1 trillion. Within five years, this number will increase by half and assets will nearly double.

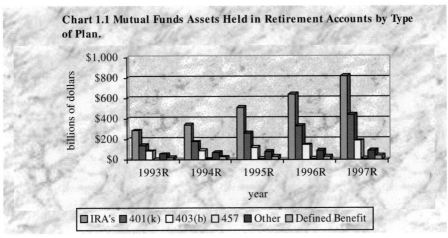

Chart 1.1 Mutual Funds Assets Held in Retirement Accounts by Type of Plan.

Source: Annual Questionnaire for Retirement Statistics,Investment Company Institute
"Other" includes profit sharing, thrift savings, stock bonus, target benefit, money purchase, and all other defined contribution plans.
"R" Revisions to 1996 data reflect corrections received to the 1996 Annual Questionnaire for Retirement Statistics. Data before 1996 were revised to incorporate information obtained from the Department of Labor, the Internal Revenue Service, and the Federal Reserve Board.

Boomers, Boomers Everywhere

Boomers have always had a huge impact on the culture. It was the Boomers who brought us the Sexual Revolution of the 1960s and 1970s. Boomers inserted the word "pot" into the national dictionary. Boomer radicals of the 1960s are often now the tenured professors and chairs of academic departments who are spawning the political correctness movement. This is true for many, but by no means all, colleges and universities.

Boomers also fought the nation's most unpopular war and generated the antimilitary attitudes that made the U.S. Army an ineffective fighting force for a decade after Vietnam. While the Boomers' parents lived through the Great Depression and fought World War II, the Boomers endured their own set of tribulations. They witnessed the first resignation of an American president. And just when many Boomers were entering the workforce, struggling to form households and start families, the stagflation of the late 1970s and the second-worst economy of the century (1980-82) dashed many aspirations.

Boomers were largely responsible for rock-and-roll. As Boomers have entered their years of relative affluence and high spending potential, it is no coincidence that the number of radio stations catering to "oldies but goodies" programming, hearkening Boomers back to the days of their youth, has more than doubled in recent years. Advertisers want their dollars to go where the numbers and the money reside.

When the First Boomers Hit Their 60s

Retirement for the majority of Americans presently takes place between the ages of 62 and 65, and is supported by the two major entitlement programs for senior citizens, Medicare and Social Security. When the Boomers reach "normal" retirement ages they will impact society, including health care, in ways which policymakers and business leaders have not yet fully considered.

Why? Boomer numbers have always caused strange things to happen to the rest of us as the Boomers have marched through life. There is no reason to believe things will be any different when the Boomers are in their twilight years. Boomer numbers are not going away.

Every American and every American institution—business, government, medicine, insurance—will have to cope with the crush of silver- and golden-year Boomers. As the Boomer "pig" reaches the end of the societal "python," the Boomers will have their last hurrah by changing the very concept of what we mean by "retirement."

Advise a son or daughter in medical school to specialize in geriatrics: the flow of patients is assured. Corporate marketing directors will scramble to reposition their products for the Boomer seniors. And who knows?—Geritol and Serutan might even make a comeback. State and local officials in popular retirement destinations (e.g., Florida and the Southwest) will have to scramble to keep up with infrastructure demands of older, but migrating Boomers. Although we argue later that Boomers will retire later than their parents—if they retire at all—many of them will nonetheless retire eventually.

It is no exaggeration to claim that the single most important social policy challenge facing us in the first half of the next century will be dealing with aging Boomers.

The demographics are stark. Often this is expressed as a coming sharp drop in the number of workers to retirees. While this is correct in terms of probabilities, it is also not the best or most reliable way to illustrate the aging Boomer problem. Those estimates are all hypothetical. They depend upon a guess as to who chooses to work and who chooses to retire. Instead, consider the pure demographics, which we cannot alter very much.

We generally consider those ages 25-64 to be in their prime and productive working years. Those 65 and older are likely candidates for wanting to be retired. What do we *know* will happen to this pool of probable workers and wannabe retirees? The answer is not pretty.

Table 1.1 The Giant Blob

Year	% Population aged 25-64	% Population aged 65+	Ratio
2000	52.1	12.6	4.1
2010	52.5	13.3	3.9
2020	51.4	16.6	3.1
2030	47.4	20.2	2.3

The ratio of those age 25 to 64 to those over 65 has been stuck at about four to one for some decades. It will stay about there through 2010. In 2011, the first Boomers (born in 1946) will reach age 65. After that, 76 million more Boomers will follow, creating a tidal wave of people reaching age 65—most looking to retire at the same time. The ratio of possible workers to probable retirees collapses. Here the ratio of prime-age workers to probable-age retirees falls from 4:1 to 3:1 by 2020, and to just above 2:1 by 2030. *It will be cut almost in half in just two decades.* The U.S. has never seen a demographic sea change approaching this magnitude.

And there isn't much we can do about it. Everyone in the U.S. who will be age 25 in 2020 is already born. Almost all of those who will be 25 or older in 2030 are already born. Barring some immediate, cataclysmic—and highly unlikely—jump in fertility rates, the estimate of a 2:3 ratio for 2030 is quite solid.

Changes in immigration policy may fiddle on the margin. Certainly there is no dearth of talented young people wanting to enter the U.S. But it would take a major shift in the political winds for immigration policy to change sufficiently to make much of a dent in this ratio. Basically we must accept the coming Boomer-driven demographic implosion as an immutable fact.

The Course of this Book

In the ensuing chapters, we discuss in detail the probable consequences of Boomer aging for health care. We will argue that they will be dramatic, so dramatic that at first blush the reader may not be inclined to accept them. Nonetheless, we argue that these health care changes are either inevitable or highly probable. Also, we will often lump Medicare and Social Security together, even though this is a book about health care. The reason is that the willingness of the young to pay for *both* must be a measure of just how much they are willing to pay to care for the elderly Boomers.

The reader will be asked to judge. We believe you will find the arguments compelling.

Before we pass on to a detailed examination of health care in 2020, we invite the reader to consider a few of the other likely implications of Boomer aging. They, too, are dramatic. Perhaps our predictions for health care for the aging Boomers will not then seem so radical after all.

The Boomers Make Their Final Strike

Aside from health care, the Boomers will force some quite remarkable changes by the year 2020. Most of these are obvious if one thinks about them.

Boomers on average will retire later, and some may not retire at all.

Boomers will shatter what we now think of as a normal retirement age.

It is easy to forget that, a century ago, there was no such thing as retirement. For most people, retirement was something for the Rockefellers, Morgans, and Guggenheims. Most people worked until they couldn't, and then hoped to have children around to take care of them.

But with the introduction of Social Security, widespread company pension plans, and rising affluence more people began to amass retirement savings and retirement became an option. Workers could spend a few years of enjoyment before death or enfeeblement. In fact, the average retirement age has been trending steadily downward for almost as far back as we have data. The average retirement age bottomed out in 1995 at just over age 62, and has risen slightly since.

Boomers will retire on average at age 70, possibly even higher. This will likely be even more true for the "young" Boomers born between 1954 and 1964, the second decade of the Baby Boom.

Delayed retirement will not be a bad thing for many Boomers. Some will voluntarily choose to work longer. Unlike workers in previous generations, fewer Boomers are in occupations requiring heavy physical labor, such as farming or manufacturing. Thus, fewer Boomers will have to quit working simply because they no longer possess sufficient physical strength. Some Boomers in knowledge industries may like what they do and be loathe to give up entirely the intellectual stimulus.

Many Boomers, however, will work longer because they have no choice. Social Security and Medicare cannot be maintained at their current levels of generosity (more on this in Chapter 2). The tax rates on the young would be confiscatory and also counterproductive since they would kill off any work incentives.

Tax rates on the young would have to rise to such levels that it is a safe bet that, even if wise (and they are not), those huge tax rates could never happen politically. Boomers with few retirement savings (and the majority have very little) and relying on Social Security and Medicare as the core of their retirement plans are doomed to serious disappointment. Social Security and Medicare will be cut back through some combination of later-than-normal retirement ages, reduced coverages and/or overt benefit cuts. Social Security will be privatized, or partially so. These changes will occur because the public budget cannot withstand continuation of the program as currently structured.

Medicare and Medicaid also cannot survive "as is." We argue in Chapter 4 that increased experimentation with, and usage of, alternative means of providing living arrangements and health care for the elderly must take place. Home health care and assisted living must become cost effective alternatives to hospitalization and full-time nursing home institutionalization.

The normal Social Security retirement age is already scheduled to gradually increase to 67 by the year 2027. Few who have examined the numbers believe this is anything but the start of a very long trend toward much higher retirement ages for federal entitlement benefits.

Social Security was once thought of as the untouchable "third rail" of American politics: touch it and you die. This is no longer the case. The political classes are quite well aware that the current system is not sustainable. Debate over how and when—not whether—to scale back Social Security has become respectable. In brief, the question is how and when to tell the Boomers and the young that they have been conned.

In this discussion, at least parts of the public are ahead of Washington. Among those under 35, nearly twice as many believe flying saucers are real as believe Social Security will amount to much by the time they are ready to retire. This assessment of probabilities is likely accurate. When politicians are ready to lead on the seniors' entitlement question, much of the public will be ready to follow.

Longer-working Boomers will create a whole additional class of problems.

The workplace will be much different with all of those Boomers hanging around longer.

Presumably many of those Boomers will be in management and supervisory positions, purely from seniority if nothing else. If business firms are not creative, those can't-or-won't-retire Boomers will clog promotion pipelines, creating resentment among their younger colleagues who will rightfully feel that they are bumping up against a "Boomer Ceiling."

Business firms may deal with this problem, but not without serious changes in employment and benefits policies. For example, old working Boomers might be shunted to off-line positions, or be asked to accept part-time employment, perhaps "employee emeritus." One thing is certain: by the year 2020, prospective employees will be grilling prospective employers about the age composition of their workforce and company policies for dealing with aged employees.

Employee benefits will also pose a challenge. Although we argue in Chapter 2 that the present tax exclusion for employment-based health insurance is certain to be repealed, some business firms will still find it useful employee relations to provide some type of health package.

But what kind?

A 70- or 75-year-old will differ greatly in his or her health care preferences from a 30-year-old. Diseases and procedures more common among the elderly—vision, hearing, joint replacement, etc.—will be popular coverages among older Boomers. In addition, many working older Boomers will have, or think they must plan to have, a very old parent for whom they must care. "Eldercare" plans will be in demand by the Boomers.

Boomers could also care less about the maternity and natal coverage prized by the young.

Employee-benefit managers will walk a very thin line trying to keep everyone happy without breaking the bank. Perhaps the line will be so thin that it cannot be walked.

Social tensions between generations are inevitable.

Boomers will eventually retire if they live long enough. The brightest, most eager old Boomer worker will some day have to admit that he or she just can't do it any more. By 2030, 2.7 million Americans will be over age 85. By then, there will be 10 million more Americans over age 65 than there will be between ages 25 and age 50. Boomer retirees will have to be taken care of *somehow*. We argue in Chapter 5 that the "bioethics" debate (just how much health care will be provided to all those old-old Boomers) is bound to reach a fever pitch.

There are no easy answers to this demographic dilemma. If the nation cannot afford every conceivable medical procedure and treatment for every single Boomer, someone or some committee must "play God" by deciding who gets what. We have had some experience with medical rationing—iron lungs and kidney dialysis machines, for example—but none of the lessons learned so far are comparable to the scope of future challenges.

Whatever retirement income and health care is provided must be provided, in some way, from current production in the year 2020. There is no way to stockpile in advance. There are not, nor will there be, warehouses filled with BMWs, Roquefort dressings, and health care professionals labeled "for the Boomers when they retire." Current workers in 2020 must provide for current retirees in 2020.

Some degree of tension between generations will occur. It cannot be avoided. As more and more oldsters make claims upon the output of the younger generations, the young are bound to feel they have been dealt a bad demographic hand. As well they have. With the shrinkage of Social Security and Medicare, many of the young may have to revert to the preentitlement era of being the primary caretakers of and providers for their elderly parents.

How this plays out is more speculative than the remainder of this book. Some resolution must take place, and, we hope, it will be nothing more than modest grumbling. But other, scarier scenarios are possible.

The young may get the upper hand and decide the very old have a bioethical "duty to die." They may refuse to pay for every conceivable medical procedure that might be of benefit for the now-geezer Boomers.

The Boomers themselves may fracture into two camps. One camp would consist of those who have stock options, or liberal 401-k and IRA plans, and who did not count on Social Security and Medicare. These will be the Boomers who made provision for their own retirement, and it is not inconceivable that they will wind up in walled compounds with private security guards. They have what others want.

The second Boomer group may be the work-until-you-drop-because-you-can't-afford-to-retire cohort. This group could be assaulted from both sides. They will envy their better off Boomer brethren, and their children and grandchildren—strapped by the financial burden of rearing the great grandchildren of these Boomers—will be hard pressed to afford the additional burden of caring for their parents.

We do not claim that this scenario will happen. We only claim that the aging Boomers will produce societal strains as powerful as this country has seen since the Slavery Question erupted into a civil war.

The Rest of the Book

This brief and nonexhaustive list of the Baby Boomer impact outside of health care should serve to establish that the Boomers will once again influence society in their aging years by their numbers alone. We now turn to what specifically the Boomers will do to health care.

CHAPTER 2
BABY BOOMERS SINK HEALTH INSURANCE
BY THE YEAR 2020

The current U.S. system of health insurance is in serious trouble and will look radically different by the year 2020. The Boomers will do it in. In this chapter, the relevance of the current health insurance system to the coming Boomer health care problem, and the entire health care financing system in year 2020 will be made clear.

The Way We Do It Now

Most working Americans and their families still receive health insurance through their place of work, but this system of predominately employment-based health insurance is crumbling under the combined assault of increased temporary employment, downsizing by major corporations, and rising costs.

Employment not covered by a health plan is increasing.

It is important to understand that when we refer to "employment-based" or "employer-provided" insurance, as opposed to "employer-paid" insurance, we do so for good reasons. Nearly every study of who really bears the ultimate cost of health insurance says it is the employee. If insurance costs the employer X dollars, in the absence of this fringe benefit that employee's cash compensation would be X higher.

If an employee making $40,000 is given $3,000 of health insurance by the employer, the employee is really paying for it. If the employer were to withdraw the health insurance benefit, the employee's cash compensation would rise by $3,000. The employee "pays" for the insurance; it just isn't obvious to him because someone else writes the check.

But the employee still benefits from the tax treatment of employment-based insurance. We will explain in detail why the current health insurance system depends upon tax treatment and why the Baby Boomer demographic will inevitably cause it to change.

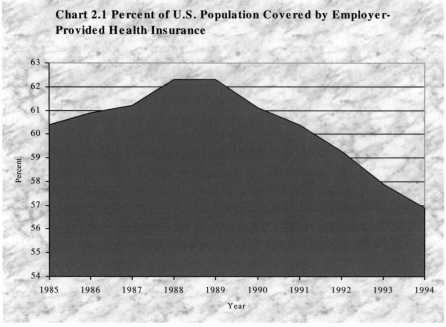

Chart 2.1 Percent of U.S. Population Covered by Employer-Provided Health Insurance

Source: Calculations from Bureau of Census, Current Population Reports, p. 29-70, 1995.

The Nature of Health Insurance

Shares of the population covered by employment-based health insurance have steadily declined since 1988. The private, individual, or family health insurance market not linked to employment remains radically distorted by differential tax treatment for employer versus individually acquired insurance.

How health insurance is acquired remains different from other types of insurance. Get fired? Or, in modern parlance, get downsized? You don't go home to your spouse and say, "Honey, I got fired. What will we do for auto insurance?" Or homeowner's insurance? Or (for the most part) life insurance. Most of us own those policies. Employment troubles may cause difficulty in maintaining premium payments, but the policies remain in force if premiums are paid. Recent policy changes (in legislation introduced by former Senator Nancy Kasselbaum [R.-Kansas], and Edward M. Kennedy [D.-Massachusetts]) have added some degree of "portability" to employment-based health insurance; but so long as health insurance is linked to employment, workers eventually run a risk of losing coverage or finding they are uninsurable or denied coverage for preexisting conditions when applying for new insurance.

Crumbling Walls?

The reason health insurance is linked to employment is simple: tax treatment. If your employer buys, or contributes to, your health insurance at the workplace, the contribution is *excluded* from your income for federal tax purposes. Check your next pay stub. If you purchase your own or family health policy, you do so with after-tax dollars. Naturally, we all would prefer that the money spent on our health insurance be exempt from taxation. (We later discuss how this bizarre arrangement came into being.)

Political support for maintaining the current tax exclusion for employment-based health insurance, which creates the tax distortion in favor of health insurance being supplied through the workplace, will inevitably

Caption: Mike Smith, USA Today

decline as fewer voters benefit.

Nor is the government side of health care financing in good shape. Government-provided health insurance faces a short-term Medicare (government health insurance for the elderly) financial crisis between the year 2008 and 2012, and more fundamental dilemmas when the first Baby Boomers reach age 65 in 2011.

The other major government health insurance program is Medicaid for welfare recipients and senior citizens. (We discuss Medicaid at greater length in Chapter 3.) As former welfare recipients become employed, at some point they will lose Medicaid as their incomes rise. There is no other choice. Two co-workers with equal incomes cannot coexist with one buying health insurance (if the firm does not have a health plan) and the other—the former welfare recipient—continuing to have government-paid health coverage. This is not a recipe for workplace harmony. Losing Medicaid thus becomes a huge stumbling block to "ending welfare as we know it." Losing Medicaid as former welfare recipients become employed also poses the risk of further increasing the number of families without any kind of health insurance. Government Kidcare programs attempt to shore up the uninsured-children problem, but as we describe in Chapter 3, Kidcare creates its own set of problems.

This chapter explores the future of health insurance as the Baby Boomers age. We review the history of employment-based health insurance and its accidental origins. In the long run, we argue that the trends will continue toward even smaller shares of the population receiving health insurance at the workplace. When the Baby Boomers begin contemplating retirement a decade hence, new political alliances—which we describe—are likely. These will make changes in the tax treatment of health insurance feasible and will open up whole new vistas in thinking about health coverage in general. These we will describe.

What is the "Uninsured" Problem?

In discussions of health insurance, there is invariably confusion over "stocks" versus "flows." There is no "stock" of permanently uninsured. People flow from one category to another. Consider just the widely discussed problem of uninsured children. The most cited number of "uninsured" children uses data from the Current Population Survey (CPS). Data from the CPS in 1993, for instance, suggests that 16 percent of all children—11.1 million—are uninsured. This could be interpreted to mean there are two groups of children out there—insured and uninsured—who are immutably in one category or another. In fact, there are significant entries and exits from both categories.

Looking at the categories of "insured" and "uninsured" through time provides a very different picture from that provided by the CPS. An alternative view comes from data from the Survey of Income and Program Participation study that followed persons and families over a thirty-two-month period (from February 1991 to September 1993). Fewer children than are suggested by the CPS data are *always* insured, and far, far fewer are *always* without health insurance. In fact, fewer than 3 percent of all children are "permanently" uninsured. About 70 percent have insurance all the time. The remaining quarter are sometimes with health insurance and sometimes without it. The number of "mostly" insured—i.e., with insurance all the time or more often than not—represents 87 percent of children under age 18.

This dynamic perspective, which sees being insured and uninsured as conditions that children (or, more precisely, their parents) move in and out of, leads to a different starting point than thinking about being insured or uninsured as permanent categories. Permanence "myopia" leads to thinking about how to solve the "uninsured" problem. In fact, the main "uninsured" problem for children is the length of time between periods when the parent(s) are insured either through employment or Medicaid.

The largest factor in creating periods of uninsurance for parents and their children is job interruption. Among 25- to 34-year-olds, 82 percent who worked continuously were always insured. In contrast, in that age group, only 53 percent of those who experienced some form of job interruption—being laid off, quitting, or otherwise not working for a time—were always insured. Job interruption on the part of parents clearly leads to periods of being without insurance among children.

Further federal legislation may, ironically, make the problem worse. If Congress requires employers to provide health coverage without preexisting-conditions exclusions, employers may, and most likely will, respond by lengthening probationary periods which new employees must serve before becoming eligible for employer-provided health benefits.

If most people who are uninsured know that they are unlikely to be forever uninsured, what does this imply? Under the assumption that most people will take "for free" what they have when they have it, it implies that consumers will time health service usage to occur during periods of insurance coverage.

There is some empirical evidence to suggest that this is exactly what people do. For example, research relating to HMOs shows higher use of services by people just joining a plan. This behavior reduces the financial risk of being uninsured, but delaying care until the next episode of insurance may have adverse health consequences.

How Did We Get Here?

Despite all of the health insurance problems we have cited, we should not forget the progress we have made. Little more than fifty years ago, few Americans had any kind of health insurance.

Prior to World War II, health insurance was uncommon. In 1940, fewer than 20 million Americans had private health insurance, mostly hospitalization coverage. Employment-based coverage was existent but rare. Many were individually purchased hospitalization policies of the Blue Cross-type, and only for routine hospitalization. There was virtually no coverage for physician care, prescription drugs, or outpatient services. No federal programs were available.

Coverage for surgical, outpatient physician and physician services not covered under hospital insurance numbered no more than several million.

"Major Medical," or catastrophic, insurance picking up large expenses not covered by other policies, was nearly nonexistent.

World War II initiated a transformation in health care financing. Faced with wartime wage controls, employers and employees sought ways to circumvent those edicts (as humans have always done when confronting price controls). One novel means was to question whether employer-provided health insurance constituted "wages" subject to the controls.

The World War II Health Insurance Anomaly

The tax treatment of health insurance is a legacy of World War II. Employers were faced with wage and price controls, and employers could not raise wages to lure additional workers into their companies. This was a particular problem in war industries where combat experience by late 1942 was indicating a need to greatly expand the production of various weapon types. In turn, this meant increased hiring in defense industries.

For example, Kaiser Shipyards needed more workers to produce transport Liberty Ships and escort vessels to defeat the German U-boats in the Atlantic. We were at that time literally "losing the war" in the North Atlantic. If Britain had been starved into submission, she would not have been available as a base for the U.S. B-17 and B-24 bombing attacks on Germany. Nor would Britain have been available as the base for the amphibious invasion of northeastern Europe in June 1944. Stalin's Soviet Union would have been left to face the might of the German Wehrmacht alone—and in pre-Stalingrad 1942 it was by no means clear that the Red Army would be up to the task. Winston Churchill wrote in his memoirs that the only time he feared the loss of the war by the Allies was during the strangling of the North Atlantic lifeline. Other war industries were screaming for more labor to produce war output.

German U-boats were literally strangling the Allies' lifeline from North America to Europe. Wage controllers, the War Labor Board, were in a box. More hiring meant higher wages to attract the necessary labor. (The other alternative, conscripting the necessary labor, was politically impossible.) If the Board started making exemptions to wage controls for certain industries, then everyone would want them, and the whole system of wage-price controls could come crumbling down. On the other hand, if they did not make exemptions, labor could not flow to the areas of desperately needed war production. The wage controllers sidestepped their dilemma neatly by ruling that increasing compensation via employers buying health insurance for employees did not constitute an increase in income to employees, and, hence, not an increase in federal taxable income.

This distinction between (taxable) income and (nontaxable) health insurance still stands today.

The Internal Revenue Service went along with this deception by ruling on 26 October 1943 that, yes indeed, employer-provided health insurance was not "income." Employer health insurance was ruled nontaxable.

High wartime tax rates (which were to persist largely after the war ended) meant that the exclusion of employer-provided health insurance from taxation was a very valuable benefit to the worker. In 1953, alarmed by the amount of revenue this tax exclusion for employment-based insurance was costing the Treasury, the IRS reversed itself and declared employer-provided health insurance to be taxable income. The next year, however, Congress overruled the IRS by voting to reinstate the exclusion.

And little wonder. By that time, Americans had grown increasingly to believe that job-related health insurance was the natural state of affairs. The war- and tax-driven push for employer-provided health insurance had conquered the political debate. By 1952, the under-20 million figure for Americans with private hospitalization insurance current in 1940 had ballooned to nearly 100 million. Citizens with surgical coverage exceeded 70 million, and those with regular physician coverage approached 40 million, both up from next to zero a mere twelve years previously.

Following Congress's 1954 reaffirmation of favored tax treatment for employer-provided health insurance, private health insurance enrollment continued to explode. By 1959, nearly 130 million were covered for hospitalization, nearly 120 million for surgical procedures, and over 80 million for regular physician expenses. At the same time, catastrophic ("Major Medical") insurance protected more than 20 million.

Nor can there be doubt that the growth in coverage came predominantly from employer- rather than individually acquired insurance or government programs. Individuals were indeed buying more health insurance, but the tax-driven rate of increase in employment-based insurance dwarfed this expansion. Business firms could deduct outlays for employee health insurance, and employees could exclude their employer's health insurance spending on them from taxable income. Individual health insurance policy purchases had to be made with employee after-tax dollars. The incentives for employees to demand, and firms to provide employer health insurance, were overpowering. In 1940, there was very little private individual health insurance. The under-20 million covered for hospitalization were almost all under employer plans. By 1960, nearly 20 million had hospitalization coverage under individual plans, and by 1970 this number was approaching 40 million. Employer group numbers, however, increased from under-20 million in 1940, to nearly 120 million in 1960, to almost 160 million in 1970.

It would be simplistic to argue that the tax treatment of health insurance was the only factor driving this expansion of employer-provided health insurance. Other factors favorable to it were also present. First, postwar prosperity generated more income for consumers to spend on everything. In 1940, personal consumption expenditures totaled $595.2 billion (in constant 1987 dollars). By 1950, 1960, and 1970 respectively this figure had increased to $874.3 billion, $1,210.8 billion, and $1,813.5 billion (205 percent). Outlays on services rose even more strongly. From $253.9 billion in 1940, services spending increased to $378.9 billion, $568.5 billion, and $912.5 billion in 1950, 1960, and 1970 respectively (259 percent).

Second, consumers had more to spend, and medicine responded with a product they would want to purchase.

Medical technology obtained an increased ability to affect patient outcomes favorably in the years following World War II. The first "miracle medical machines"—iron lungs for polio patients—were in widespread use. The first "miracle drugs"—penicillin and sulfonamides—were saving lives. In the 1940-1965 period, hospital beds increased by 85 percent. Physicians per 100,000 population rose from 133 to 153. The nursing profession expanded even more dramatically, from 216 to 319 per 100,000 population.

Americans had, for the first time, some reason other than hope and faith in a kindly doctor to believe medicine could make a real difference.

The combination of more money to spend (and therefore more income to protect), and better but more expensive medical care (which raised the financial stakes involved in the probability of prolonged medical treatment) drove the trend to health insurance. Per capita out-of-pocket spending rose in the 1948-1958 decade from $40 to $60 per capita. Medical outlays covered by insurance began that decade at a few dollars per capita, but by 1958 were approaching $20 per head of population. The insurance component of health care spending was trailing but gaining ground fast. And with about three-quarters of covered individuals in employer-provided plans, it was the employer market leading the way.

Some Consequences of the Tax Treatment of Health Insurance

Federal tax policy creates a huge incentive for employees to receive health insurance through their employers. The employer deducts the insurance cost from taxable income and is indifferent as to whether a dollar of compensation is paid out as wages and salaries or as health insurance premiums.

The employee, however, is by no means indifferent. Employer-provided health insurance is excluded from income. But most econometric studies of the incidence of health insurance indicate that the cost is "back-shifted" to the employee. That is, in the absence of health insurance costing X, the employee's wages and salaries would rise by X. Without employer-provided health insurance, the employee would be forced to pay taxes on X and acquire insurance on his or her own with after-tax dollars. The value of the tax subsidy to employer-provided health insurance is the foregone revenue on untaxed health insurance premiums. Estimates of this value range from 15 to 24 percent of the premiums. In dollar terms, this is a huge figure. In 1975, it may have been as low as $3.5 billion. In 1994, the subsidy was $58.4 billion. It will increase to $96.3 billion by the year 2000. By the year 2020, we can only guess at the amount.

The effect of any subsidy is to raise the quantity (and usually price) of the good or service demanded. We would expect *a priori* more health insurance to be demanded from employers than would be the case without the subsidy. Economist Martin Feldstein, a former Director of the National Bureau of Economic Research and former Chairman of the President's Council of Economic Advisors, argued that the effect is multifaceted. Not only are more employees covered, but more medical services are covered. Out-of-pocket expenses (co-pays, deductibles) are reduced, thus tending to make medical care a (near) "free good" with obvious implications for utilization of the service. He also argued that a "supply side" effect existed. The hospital sector acquired ever more technologically sophisticated (and expensive) equipment and beefed up their staffs as a means of competing for doctors and patients. While this may have led to better quality of care, it also generated "cost-push" pressures on health care and insurance prices. Higher health care costs raised the price (potential loss) of an uninsured medical episode, leaving more consumers unwilling to do without health insurance.

It is sometimes argued that health care costs are a kind of perpetual motion machine. Consumers always desire the "best" quality care. They would purchase the same amount and quality of health care regardless of price, whether in the form of a tax subsidy to employment-based insurance or not.

Available evidence suggests otherwise. A RAND Corporation experiment divided subjects into four different classes based on insurance plans ranging from zero percent coinsurance to very high coinsurance percentages. Utilization of both physician and hospital services by the lowest co-pay group was higher than the highest co-pay group by more than half. Some experiments with Medical Savings Accounts (which we discuss at length in later chapters), in which employees own any unspent balances at the end of the year, also report some evidence of lower utilization rates for some categories of medical services. An accident victim carried unconscious to an emergency room is in no position to "shop around," but many routine medical goods and services such as prescription drugs and many outpatient services respond to competitive pressure if consumers are willing to apply it.

It is not only that consumers do not "shop" when they have generous employer-provided insurance. They do not even regard these outlays as "their" money. They think that it is paid for "by my employer." This will change. And it will change with a vengeance when the Baby Boomers start asking their retirement questions.

The Long Run: The Coming Unraveling of Employer-Provided Health Insurance

Following a four-decade-long growth after World War II, the share of the population covered by employer-provided health insurance peaked in 1988, and has been in persistent decline since then. We reproduce this chart from *Health United States,* U.S. Public Health Service. It is crucial to comprehending the shrinking population share covered.

In what was formerly a "growth" industry, the share of the population receiving health insurance through their or a family-member's place of employment has dropped by nearly a tenth in less than a decade. Moreover, there are sound reasons to believe the share will decline further, then collapse completely when the Baby Boomers begin retiring in the second decade of the next century. This will have profound implications for the health care financing system.

Consider the contributing factors to this phenomenon of ever-smaller shares of the U.S. population covered by employment-based insurance, none of which have as yet completely run its course:

Corporate Downsizing/Outsourcing

IBM's shedding of 154,000 employees over a four-year period makes news, as does AT&T's laying off of 45,000 employees and Apple Computer's recent efforts to survive by paring payrolls. But the phenomenon has also been pervasive across larger companies. In the last thirteen years Fortune 1000 companies have decreased full-time employment by nearly 4 million. Smaller firms have added 24 million jobs, but smaller firms are far less likely to offer health insurance as part of their compensation package. Larger firms offer some kind of health insurance to 83 percent of their employees; for small firms, the figure drops to only 69 percent. The gap is not large for professional and technical (i.e., upper income) employees, where 85 percent of large company employees and 82 percent of smaller company employees are covered. However,

Table 2.1
Percent of U.S. Population Covered by
Employer-Provided Health Insurance

Year	Percent
1985	60.4
1986	60.9
1987	61.2
1988	62.3
1989	62.3
1990	61.1
1991	60.4
1992	59.3
1993	57.9
1994	56.9

Source: Calculations from Bureau of the Census, Current Population
Reports, p 29-70, 1995.
Note: This is a tabular form of Chart 2.1, but bears repeating.

the gap widens to 81 percent versus 75 percent for clerical and sales workers, and widens further to 84 percent versus 60 percent for production and service workers. That is, lower income employees who are least likely to afford to buy health insurance on their own are also the least likely to have employer-provided health insurance if employed by a smaller firm.

Downsizing by large firms will continue. Downsizing passes the "market test." Firms' share prices continue to rise on news of downsizing, signaling that the markets still believe larger firms have "too many" employees. Corporate mergers, which typically result in higher stock prices for one or both firms, also produce layoffs as redundant staff are eliminated. We will know downsizing is at an end when share prices drop on news of layoffs and attrition-based job loss, signaling that markets believe the productive core of the company is being cut. That time is not yet at hand, and the shift of employment from large to small firms will continue to contribute modestly to the declining share of the population that receives health insurance from employers. At the time of this writing, stock prices worldwide are generally declining because of fallout from the Asian/Russian/South American financial meltdown. Share prices of U.S. firms, particularly those which have downsized, are generally rising.

The Rise of the Temporary Worker

Also contributing to the declining population share with employer-provided health insurance is a dramatic rise in temporary employment. Some employees of organized temporary service companies have employer-provided health insurance, but most do not (in some cases, coverage may be available through a spouse). Temporary employment is the fastest growing segment of the labor force by an order of magnitude. The organized temporary service employment market grew from 1.16 million in 1992 to 1.74 million in 1994 (first quarter to first quarter). This 51 percent increase swamped the 3 percent increase in full-time employment by an order of magnitude, and then some. Temporary employment was adding 300,000 jobs per year and providing a sizable fraction of employment growth.

It was also driving down shares of the population with health insurance coverage. Temporary employment is more prevalent in small business, and 43 percent of temporary employment is in the office-clerical category, the category least likely to have employer-provided insurance.

The factors fueling the rapid growth of temporary employment are unlikely to abate. The data indicate large companies are even likelier than usual historically to be reluctant to add full-time employees, preferring to cycle in temporary or seasonal workers. The persistently recurring trend toward more employment in smaller companies is also a factor. A very small business may have no need for a full-time clerical employee and opt for an ongoing part-timer. Nor is the supply of temporary workers likely to shrink as "better" jobs with health insurance become available. While some temporary workers view temporary employment as a "bridge" to full-time employment, a large majority (61 percent) do not.

Public policy also contributes. Whatever the merits of the Earned Income Tax Credit (EITC), in its current form it creates a large disincentive for low earners to work more and make more income. Families under the EITC face a marginal tax rate of 21 percent from the phase out of the EITC as earnings grow, plus a 7.65 percent Social Security payroll tax, another 7.65 percent "paid" by the employer, plus income taxes—a total marginal tax rate of 49 percent. This is a powerful incentive to forego full-time employment (and higher earnings) for part-time work.

A second public policy encouragement for temporary employment is the small business "thresholds" for bringing businesses under various federal social policy laws. Small business has succeeded politically in exempting firms below certain employment levels from coverage. For example, the marginal cost to a small business with forty-nine employees of hiring the fiftieth employee is not the cost of salaries and benefits necessary to attract that employee. The rational owner will also add an estimate for what it might cost the firm to be covered by the Civil Rights Act (CRA). The fiftieth employee is the tripwire that engages the CRA. Similar tripwires are at the twentieth employee (Age Discrimination Act), fiftieth employee (Americans with Disabilities Act and the Family Leave Act), and hundredth employee (Business Closing Act). At each of these hurdles, the rational small business owner will think twice and thrice before hiring a full-time employee, particularly as he is apt to overestimate the potential cost of bringing his business under the new law because of unfamiliarity with the law and the resultant uncertainty. One common strategy is to cycle in temporary workers and only as a last resort hire the tripwire full-time employee. None of this is to argue that these laws are necessarily "bad," only that they create a barrier to growth in full-time employment and a strong encouragement for temporary hiring.

Temporary employment is unlikely to go away as a contributor to a smaller share of Americans who have employer-provided health insurance.

Medical Cost Inflation

Rapidly rising medical prices in the 1980s and early 1990s, often at double-digit rates, evoked a two-stage response by business. First, many companies asked their employees to accept higher deductibles and co-pays. Second, many turned to managed care. Currently, the rapid rise in medical costs has abated, but many analysts expect the rise to return to double digits in a few years once the managed care "fix" has worked its way as far as it can through the system.

It May Already Be Happening

This viewpoint—that medical prices are once again trending upward—is gaining wider currency. Some 85 percent of private-sector working Americans are now covered by managed care plans. There is little remaining room to add new enrollees. Largely because of this factor, in September 1998 the Health Care Financing Administration forecast total U.S. health care spending would double by 2007, from $1.035 trillion in 1996 to $2.133 trillion in 2007. Health spending as a share of GDP will rise from 13.3 percent to 16.6 percent of GDP. While no forecast of this type can be expected to be precise, it nonetheless represents a credible projection of where we are likely to go.

In 2007, the oldest Boomer will be a relatively young 61 years of age. Where will this trend go when the Boomers begin getting very old and become heavy consumers of health care in the last year(s) of their lives? Any projection that far out carries some risk. In the absence of any of the policy and attitudinal changes we describe elsewhere, a minimum of 20 percent of GDP is a certainty, and 25 percent or higher could occur—possibly much higher if medical technology advances should move generally in the direction of better but costlier treatments for currently treatable diseases, and new treatments for currently untreatable diseases. It is precisely the question of whether society, especially the young, would be willing to tolerate such levels of spending that cause us to ask the questions posed in this book.

What strategy will business employ then to cope with rising health-benefit costs? The "easy" fixes have already been implemented. The answers are necessarily speculative. However, one can easily foresee more firms moving to a "defined contribution" plan (as is already occurring with retirement plans) by capping the amount of, or the rate of increase in, what they will spend for each employee for health insurance, and asking the employee to make a greater contribution toward his or her health benefits. To the extent some employees are unwilling to pay more, they will still have coverage, but it will be insurance inferior to what they had before.

But if medical inflation does experience a resurgence, some firms may also adopt a "been there, done that, and never again" attitude toward health coverage for their employees. They may simply stop—call everyone in, explain how much is being spent on their health insurance, explain how the company cannot go on paying for it, and offer to increase their wage compensation by that amount. A rational employee, skilled in the arcana of economics literature, will know about the back-shifting of employer health insurance outlays and regard this as a bad deal. But not every employee is rational. Some families, particularly younger, lower earning, cash-strapped families, may have a very high rate of "discount" between a sizable additional chunk of cash in the pay envelope versus vague medical expenses in the future, and accept the offer. In the sense that they voluntarily take the deal, their behavior is "rational." But it will increase the percentage of the uncovered population.

What Does All This Mean?

The foregoing discussion demonstrates in some detail why the U.S.

health insurance system, and any analysis which seeks to discuss the coming retirement problems of the Baby Boomers, should be considered in a dynamic light. Measures that are "unthinkable" and considered politically impossible now may become quite thinkable in five or ten years.

It may be that only trivial changes are possible in the short run. If downsizing and the trend toward temporaries continue, and if medical inflation resumes its lofty pace, then fewer voters will have a fond attachment to the current employment-based health insurance system. A smaller share of the population will be covered, and those who remain so will be less well-covered. The growing ranks of the health insurance uncovered will be demanding public policy action of almost any kind.

And a little over ten years down the road almost anything is thinkable because of—

2011: The Medicare Collapse

In 2011, the first Baby Boomers will reach age 65. That's a mere twelve years, less than the span since the Iran-Contra mess engulfed Ronald Reagan. Not at all a long time in public policy evolution. Medicare will be facing a tremendous financial strain in the future. And this assumes Medicare can be cured of its short-run financial problems. Medicare ran a small deficit in 1995, earlier than expected, and is now projected to hit zero balances in the Trust Fund in May 2008 or slightly later. So far, the nation has not mustered the political will to resolve a comparatively trivial short-run problem that pales when compared to the decisions that will have to be made another decade down the road.

Behind the initial Boomers will come a tidal wave of people. The numbers are familiar, but we will mention them. The 45-year-old population cohort of 1991 numbers 2.8 million; the 44-year-old cohort of 1991, nearly 4 million. Behind them are cohorts exceeding 4 million.

The impact of this demographic shift on how heath care is financed cannot be underestimated. It is close at hand, and it will render all current customs and thinking obsolete.

For example, it may seem paradoxical that pressures on health care for the elderly will greatly impact measures for health care for children. Nonetheless, that will be the case (see Chapter 3). It will happen because the Boomer-driven collapse of Medicare will tear loose the moorings of the current employer-provided health insurance system, leaving room for a complete rethinking of how medical care is financed in the U.S.

Presently, the share of retirees who receive some kind of employer-based health care insurance looks, if not robust, at least noncataclysmic.

This is deceptive. About 51 percent of persons in the age 65-69 bracket in 1987 had employment-based health insurance through their present or former employer. In the age 70-74 bracket, the number dropped to 44 percent. This was while the share of the population receiving employment-based health insurance was at its peak. These shares of covered population drop off as compared to working employees (even in smaller business), but they do not alarmingly go to something approaching zero. Of the remainder, of the over-55 retirement population, 32 percent had privately

Chart 2.2 *The Ratio of the Prime Working Age Population to the Elderly is Falling*

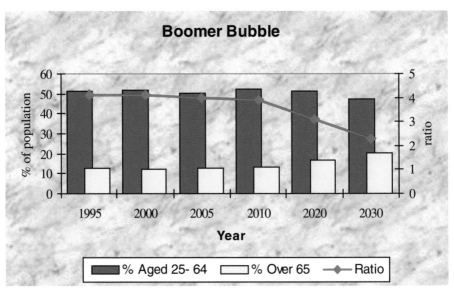

Source: Census Brueau projections.

purchased coverage, but 19 percent did not.

Except that these numbers about retirees getting health insurance by reason of past or present employment (i.e., "retired" from a former job, but employed elsewhere) work with the current Medicare system. Mostly they deal with "Medigap" or Medicare Supplement policies. What if "Medicare-as-we-know-it" isn't around?

Medicare-as-we-know-it is highly unlikely to be around when the Boomers start to retire. The Boomers are at the back end of a demographic chain letter, and they know it.

Estimates of what increases in payroll taxes would be required to maintain the current Medicare (not to mention Social Security) system when the Boomers retire vary wildly with predictions of future economic growth and medical costs, but it is a safe generalization that they all would relegate the children of the Boomers to the category of high-taxed serfs: perhaps 51 percent of payroll by 2030, plus federal income taxes and state and local taxes on top. These are confiscatory levels that may cause the Boomers' children to rebel.

Boomer Jones

Consider what the thinking of the Baby Boomers is likely to be as 2011 approaches. Consider Boomer Jones.

He begins to contemplate retirement seriously. By this time, the stark realities of the demographics are reaching the popular press. The Kerry Commission Report of 1995—from a commission co-chaired by Senators Robert Kerry (D.-Kansas) and John Danforth (R.- Missouri) that questioned whether Medicare and Social Security can be maintained in their current form—is beginning to look downright prophetic. Government-supplied Medicare is looking to be a weak reed on which to base future plans for retirement health insurance. Those employers who in the past might have been willing to chip in for post-retirement Medicare supplement coverage balk at the notion of being the future primary health insurance suppliers for their soon-to-be former (and unproductive) employees.

Boomer Jones sees no very comprehensive government-supplied health insurance can be had without bankrupting his children. He sees no (or at least limited) post-retirement health insurance from an employer who, in any case, has by now been relegated by the factors discussed above to a minority of employers who provide health insurance even to their working employees. He knows instinctively that the sheer numbers of his fellow Boomers and (by now) their senior positions at the commanding heights of business and politics allow them latitude to make sweeping changes not previously "thinkable." He may ponder a government-run, single-payer, universal coverage model, but he likely will reject such a government health "guarantee" through distrust of government promises in general.

Government single-payer health insurance will not seem to be a good deal to Boomer Jones. After all, the Social Security promise of a certain retirement income will be being reneged upon, or greatly scaled back, at about the same time. Boomer Jones will feel greatly put upon, and may look around and notice that government-supplied health care has never delivered on its promises, whether in the U.K., the U.S., Canada, or elsewhere.

The Boomers will look for ways to make the private health insurance market work better. What other choices have they?

Reexamine the Tax Exclusion

An alliance of the uninsured (and their children), and the Boomer Joneses beginning to contemplate retirement seriously (say, those 50 and older) but without much in the way of employer- or government-supplied health insurance, will begin to examine the irrationality of the current tax treatment of employer-provided health insurance. What they will find is a policy with nothing to recommend it.

No one decided that allowing employers to deduct the cost of health insurance and simultaneously allowing employees to exclude this as income was a particularly "good" way to finance health insurance. It was an historical World War II quirk that never would have emerged from an upfront debate over "What's the best way to organize the health insurance market?"

The exclusion is arguably the single most regressive part of the federal income tax. The effect is twofold. Upper-income employees tend to take a greater share of their compensation in benefits rather than salary. Thus, a generous (and expensive) health insurance package is excluded as income at a high marginal tax rate. Lower paid employees tend to have less generous health insurance (or none at all) and exclude it against a low marginal tax rate. Families with incomes of $20,000 receive far less than one-fifth the subsidy of families earning $100,000.

The exclusion puts smaller companies, everything else being equal, at a disadvantage against larger firms. Smaller firms have much higher underwriting and marketing expenses for health insurance coverage than larger firms.

The health insurance income tax exclusion restricts consumer choice. The differential tax treatment effectively herds employees into whatever health package the firm's benefits manager negotiates with insurance companies. (How many employees reject their employer-provided insurance with a "No, thank you—I'd rather buy my own"?) Employer-provided health insurance is tax-driven, community-rated corporate paternalism.

The young and healthy are cross-subsidizing the older, potentially sicker employees without their consent or, indeed, even their knowledge. Their younger medical profiles, less likely on average to demand expensive medical interventions, reduce the risk of the employer group as a whole.

The exclusion is unlimited, thus promoting the purchase of more health insurance than the individual would want without it.

The exclusion distorts the health insurance market, encouraging the majority (at the moment) to receive their health insurance at the place of work, and thus leaving the nonemployer market small, less competitive, and more expensive than otherwise.

The exclusion locks employees into jobs they would like to leave but can't or won't because of the real or imaginary fear of being denied insurance for a preexisting condition.

And, to state the obvious, when the primary delivery vehicle for health insurance is the employer, the employer creates the enormous anxiety of the employee being without health insurance just when the employee is least able to afford the alternatives—when out of work.

The Politics of Repealing/Capping the Health Insurance Tax Exclusion

Present retirees and pre-retirees do not much think about these drawbacks in the tax treatment of health insurance. They have no reason to do so. They have Medicare (probably) for the foreseeable future, and by paying an average of $1,700 per year they can buy Medicare Supplemental insurance to cover the holes in Medicare coverage. But Medicare is rather bad health insurance—it does not cover many things. If one travels outside the U.S., for example, Medicare is nonexistent, unless you are traveling through Canada between the lower forty-eight states and Alaska. Have a heart attack at the top of the Eiffel Tower, though, and you're not covered.

Regardless, most oldsters still regard Medicare as the Holy Grail of health insurance. They're taken care of, or so they think.

But in a Few More Years—

Little more than a decade hence, that will not be the case. It should be possible to build an overpowering political coalition to repeal or severely restrict the health insurance exclusion. Not only possible, but something bordering on inevitable.

The share of the population receiving employer-provided insurance will be lower and the defenses of employer-provided insurance in general weaker, but there are also identifiable groups who can be enlisted.

The Coalition to Repeal: The Boomers

First will be the Boomers themselves. When they retire—or want to— they will no longer benefit from the health insurance tax exclusion. By definition, they will not have an employer. Medicare will be, or be about to become, a shadow of what it is today. The option of work until you die just to have health insurance will not be attractive. A repeal or capping of the exclusion, coupled with a tax credit or voucher to help with the purchase of health insurance, makes the Boomers obvious winners.

The Coalition to Repeal: Business

A large part of the business community will sign up. They will see this as an alternative to the mounting pressures to make them the primary suppliers of expensive retiree health insurance.

The Coalition to Repeal: The Left

The Left could can be swayed by noting the highly regressive nature of the tax treatment of health insurance. Repealing or capping the exclusion would result in an income distribution far more to their liking.

The Coalition of Repeal: The Right

The Right could buy in with the argument that taxing all income above a personal exemption level once, but only once, is a cardinal principle of the flat tax.

The Coalition to Repeal: The Young

Finally, it is quite conceivable that the young could be made supportive of, or at least acquiescent to, a Grand Compact between generations. When the Social Security/Medicare chain letter unwinds, someone is going to get hurt. They may prefer to relinquish their health insurance tax subsidy (over half of the young will likely not be receiving the health insurance subsidy by then in any case) in exchange for an escape from the crushing tax rate increases necessary to "rescue" Medicare.

Meshing with the Flat Tax

Major changes in the federal tax structure rarely occur in isolation. Repealing or capping the exclusion for employer-provided health insurance certainly qualifies as "major." To pass a major change in the tax code, one needs to bundle it with other major changes favored by other interests in a major bill making many changes. One intriguing concept is to mesh major surgery on the health insurance tax exclusion in a "flat tax" concept. (We do not claim this is necessarily the only feasible package involving the exclusion, only that it fits particularly well.)

A flat tax is a simple concept. Give everyone a large personal exemption

($30,000 of income is often mentioned) and tax all income above that level at a lower universal rate. A rate of 17 percent or 19 percent would raise about the same amount of money as does the current federal income tax, with its large numbers of deductions and credits.

Every major tax reform plan recently advanced eliminates the tax break for employer-provided health insurance. The consumption tax ideas put forward by Senators Richard Lugar (R.-Indiana), Peter Domenici (R.-New Mexico), former Senator Sam Nunn (D.-Georgia) and Representative Bill Archer (R.-Texas), Chairman of the House Ways and Means Committee, do so by definition. They totally eliminate the federal income tax. The flat taxes proposed by presidential candidate Steve Forbes and Representative Dick Armey (R.-Texas) eliminate the deduction that business is allowed. So do the original flat tax proposals written by various economics professors many years ago. The "flatter" tax proposed by Representative Richard Gephardt (D.-Missouri), House Minority leader, ends the exclusion from employee income. Most rank-and-file flat tax supporters have not balked at the elimination of the health insurance exclusion but have listed mortgage interest deductions and charitable contributions as their preferred "addbacks" to deductions.

The health insurance tax exclusion is vulnerable even on current political grounds. We believe a flat or flatter tax with serious changes in the exclusion for employer-provided health insurance is an idea whose time will soon come. There are simply too many irrationalities and economic growth-killing elements in the current federal income tax for it to stand much longer as it is.

Yet simply eliminating the exclusion as part of a flat tax, in the absence of other policy actions, does little to extend health insurance coverage. In the short run, it will result in less coverage, as employers would presumably convert the health insurance payments to cash wages and invite employees to purchase their own (in the case of removing the employer deduction), or employees would no longer demand health insurance as a routine condition of employment (in the case of removing the exclusion from employee income). The Congressional Budget Office (CBO) has estimated that the number of Americans without health insurance might rise by on the order of 20 percent.

While it might be argued, correctly, that over a very long period of time the CBO estimate is shortsighted and that additional economic growth from lower marginal tax rates coupled with increased competition in the nonemployer private insurance market would eventually rectify this, there can be little doubt that the short- to medium-term effect of repeal of the health insurance tax exclusion will be to reduce coverage.

Expanding Health Insurance Coverage

If the objective is to expand health insurance coverage, other measures must be coupled with repeal of the exclusion, and the $100 billion in federal revenues about to be foregone by the exclusion repeal must be used to finance these other measures. These measures must also be "universal" to retain the support of the Baby Boomers (in effect, a political alliance between the powerless uninsured and their even more powerless children, and the potent, soon-to-be uninsured Boomers). Flat tax advocates would have to accept a modestly higher tax rate (approximately 3-4 percentage points) if revenue from the exclusion is not available for rate cuts.

For this discussion we use a figure of $130 billion from repeal of the exclusion, rather than the oft-cited $100 billion figure. We will assume states adjust their own income tax bases to conform to the federal change. (Only a handful of the states, the largest being Texas, do not have a state income tax. Of the states with income taxes, a minority "piggyback" their state taxable income to federal taxable income. However, to avoid administrative complexity, a large majority of the others define state adjusted gross income as federal adjusted gross income as of a specific date, with few additions or deletions, and periodically update their state tax codes to conform to federal changes. This will add approximately $30 billion to the revenue increase.)

We will limit discussion of "other measures" to those that can be financed by repealing or limiting the exclusion for employer-provided health insurance. Any increase of general federal taxes in the foreseeable future seems to us neither likely (nor desirable).

Option 1: Increase the Personal Allowance

Every flat tax proposal has a high level of personal allowance based upon some estimate of exempting sufficient income from tax to feed, clothe, and shelter the family. Based upon an assumed marginal tax rate of 23 percent and a population of 260 million, outright repeal of the exclusion would allow a $500-per-person credit (refundable) or an increase in the personal deduction of perhaps $3,000.

But simply increasing the personal deduction will do little to expand health insurance coverage.

Children without health insurance likely have parents temporarily unemployed. Whatever income their parents may have is already shielded from taxation under most flat tax plans extant.

A universal credit holds more promise. A retired Boomer couple will have an extra $1,000 to spend, on health insurance (or anything else). They are

$1,000 better off, as repeal of the exclusion has cost them nothing. (To the objection that many retirees are better off than current workers and that this is questionable social policy, our answer would be, Yes, but, sweeping changes in tax treatment of health insurance are impossible without Boomer political support).

A $500-per-capita refundable credit would make $2,000 available to each family of four. That also happens to be almost exactly the average cost of a high-deductible nonemployer policy. Repeal of the exclusion coupled with a tax credit would make most families financially able to afford high-deductible health insurance. Mechanisms could be devised for the insurer to apply for an "early refund" to pay for all or most of the policy to tide the family over until actually filing a return.

Option 2: Per Capita Credit Conditioned on Purchase of Insurance

A "$500-for-everybody" plan with no strings attached may seem unsatisfying. To some it may smack of a George McGovern giveaway. To others it may seem insufficiently directed toward a worthy goal.

The credit could be conditioned on spending at least the amount of the credit on the purchase of health insurance. Since the credit would be less than the cost of almost all health insurance policies marketed, it would trigger at an either/or, have bought/have not bought health insurance threshold. The insurer would send the purchaser what amounts to a reverse IRS Form 1099 to certify purchase. The taxpayer would receive the income tax credit as an offset to the health insurance purchase.

To avoid the regressive nature of the current subsidy, the health insurance credit should not vary with the amount spent on health insurance.

Option 2 would target repeal of the exclusion to alternative private purchase of insurance.

Option 2 would also require a discussion of the premise of this paper. Is universal health insurance coverage for future Baby Boomer retirees the objective? Or is the objective enhancing voluntary coverage by improving the ability of currently uninsured households to get health care coverage?

Option 2 clearly would result in more insured persons than Option 1. However, there is no way to ensure universal insurance without a public mandate. Any such government edict violates the most basic tenets of voluntary exchange.

Option 3: Credit Combined with Medical Savings Accounts

Medical Savings Accounts are a simple concept. They rely on the individual or family, rather than a third-party payer such as the employer-contracted insurance company or the government, to make medical payment decisions. Purchase a high-deductible insurance policy to take care of catastrophic medical expenses, then make a tax-free deposit to take care of medical expenses up to (or close to) the deductible amount of the insurance policy.

This gives equal tax treatment to individual and employment-based health insurance. Both are tax exempt.

In the public debate, MSAs are usually thought to benefit only those employed. Employers buy a catastrophic policy and give the remainder of what they would have spent on employee health insurance to employees for deposit in their MSAs. Employees have first-dollar coverage up to the amount in their MSAs, and pay any remaining medical expenses out of pocket up to the deductible under the catastrophic policy. Suppose, however, we had a regime under which a tax credit financed by repeal of the tax exclusion for employer-provided insurance provided enough financial resources, on average, for a catastrophic policy for the family, and employers added taxable cash to employee compensation in lieu of health insurance. This should average perhaps $2,000 for the "savings account" portion of the MSA per family after taxes. On average, all citizens could afford a $3000 deductible health insurance policy financed by their government credit from the health insurance.

Why "On Average" Is Dangerous

"On average" is a mathematically precise but politically elusive term, particularly when it comes to any discussion of the political possibilities for any major changes in federal tax policy. Almost no voter is "average." The cost of any life or health insurance policy rises with age, for reasons everyone understands. The probability of a claim rises with age. The cost of a high-deductible policy for a healthy 23-year-old is trivial. The cost for a 90-year-old for a similar policy would be—well, we don't know because as the result of Medicare such policies are not issued now, but that cost would be many times in excess of the $400 or $500 credit were everyone to receive the same amount.

A Slightly Modified Credit

Nonetheless, if repeal of the exclusion would make sufficient resources available for a universal credit for purchase of high-deductible health insurance, simple arithmetic dictates there must be a way to make a similar health insurance policy available for both the 23-year-old and the 90-year-old.

We surveyed currently offered "high-deductible" policies for 64-year-olds. (Private insurance, except for "Medigap" policies, is not a product insurance companies find attractive right now because Medicare is still in place for those 65 and over.) The policies offered for 64-year-olds exceed the per capita amounts which could be made available by repeal of the current health insurance tax exclusion. When Medicare is no longer what it is today, as we argue is inevitable when Boomers begin to reach age 65 in large numbers, high-deductible insurance products for those over 64—though increasingly expensive—will become attractive for private insurance companies to invent, if only the Boomer elderly can pay for them.

One intriguing possibility would be a "sliding scale" with the amount of the tax credit rising with age. The young would get a few hundred dollars, the "young-old" slightly under $1,000, and the very old several thousand dollars. The precise amounts would have to be determined by actuaries after the Medicare collapse and private insurance companies enter the market for the post-64-year-olds.

A "Reverse" Medical Savings Account

This scenario is a sort of "reverse" MSA. Instead of "leveling the health insurance playing field" by extending the tax exclusion to MSAs, as the current MSA debate envisions, we implicitly assume here that the current push for widely available tax-exempt MSAs will not be successful. (Answering the question of whether this failure would be a good thing or bad thing is not necessary for this discussion.) We argue instead that the playing field will be eventually leveled in any case—by making both taxable. Repeal of the exclusion makes sufficient resources available for the purchase of catastrophic insurance, and many employers will choose eventually to drop out of the health insurance business by giving their employees taxable cash—a combination of circumstances that makes MSAs quite feasible.

Summary Conclusions

Millions of persons are without any health insurance protection. Over a period of time, several times that many are uninsured at least part of the time. But the coming of the Boomers will unravel the bizarre system of private health insurance based mostly on the workplace.

People are uninsured largely because their health insurance is closely tied to the workplace. Employment-based health insurance still dominates the health insurance market. People are uninsured when they are out of work or working for an employer not offering health benefits, or are unwilling or unable to purchase other private insurance.

The dominance of employment-based health insurance stems from attempts by employers to increase compensation while not raising wages to avoid World War II-style wage controls. It is attractive to the employee because insurance provided by the employer is excluded from the employee's taxable income. Other private insurance must be paid for with after-tax dollars.

Employment-based insurance was a huge growth in the postwar years. However, this trend peaked in the late 1980s. The share of the population covered by employment-based insurance has been in steady decline since. With further downsizing of major corporations, a trend toward temporary workers, and a probable resurgence of medical price inflation, there is every reason to believe this trend toward an ever-smaller share of the population covered by employment-based health insurance will continue.

As this trend continues, political support for maintaining the employment-based health insurance tax exclusion will erode. An ever-smaller share of the electorate will benefit. When the Baby Boomers begin contemplating retirement toward the end of the next decade, it will collapse completely. A powerful coalition can, and will be, assembled to repeal the exclusion.

With repeal of the exclusion, a number of options for expanding health insurance will open up. (Those options do not have to be meshed with a "flat tax" plan, but they mesh particularly well in concept.) Repeal of the exclusion (making employment-based insurance taxable), coupled with the return of those increased federal tax dollars to each American, would put at least high-deductible health insurance within reach of almost every family and individual. This could be achieved through a variety of systems of various kinds of refundable tax credits. As more employers decide to be less generous in the health insurance for their employees—or decide to drop it altogether—Medical Savings Accounts will become an attractive option for many, but especially the young.

Americans under the age of 75 or 80 think of health insurance through the place of employment as being the natural state of affairs—they have never known anything else. Yet it is not. It is a relic of World War II. Employment-based health insurance is an historical accident. Once our thinking leaps out of the box labeled "We do it this way because we have always done it this way," many other arrangements superior to employment-based insurance can be discussed. One of them will be adopted. We are certain the exclusion will be repealed by a coalition of the Boomers, business, the Left, the Right, and at least some of the young. The most likely replacement is a universal credit for health insurance purchase that will encourage the widespread use of Medical Savings Accounts. But health insurance in the year 2020 will look nothing like it does today. Boomers will force sweeping changes.

CHAPTER 3
KIDCARE: POSSIBILITIES AND DANGERS

Introduction

We argue in this book that the Baby Boomers will transform the way we finance and provide health care in America. In addition to altering the nature of employer-provided programs for adults and forcing changes in the way government-provided Medicare is financed and delivered to older Americans, the changes the Boomers will bring to health care will directly impact the health care of children as well.

America's children, who through no fault of their own are sometimes left without access to health care coverage, should not be left stranded in the health care system of the year 2020. People of all political and ideological stripes share this common interest in getting America's children access to health care services.

While data indicate that the vast majority of America's children are very healthy most of the time, the small proportion of children who for whatever reason have trouble accessing high-quality health services when they need them is a very real public policy issue. And when our employer-provided health care system crashes, this problem may get worse. The policy challenge is to expand access to quality health care for all of America's children while at the same time making adequate health care provisions for the multitudes of Boomers.

As we argued in Chapter 2, as the result of systemic and irreversible changes in American society—the demographic time bomb of aging and retiring Boomers, a continuing explosion of temporary and contingent workers, and an increase in small business growth—the current employment-provided health care system will be in shambles by the year 2020. Of course, companies will always entice highly productive employees with generous benefits, but by 2020 most Americans will receive neither generous benefits nor health care insurance directly from their employers.

This fundamental shift away from an employer-provided system in the health care delivery system market will have a major impact on children's health care. When Mom and Dad are no longer receiving generous family health care benefits from their employers, we will have to look elsewhere to provide health care services to America's children.

It is morally unacceptable if, in our advanced society, a single American child is unable to access quality health care services. But America's health care insurance system by 2020 will be fundamentally different from what it is today—which could mean a deterioration in children's ability to receive high-quality health care services.

A recent federally mandated child health care program—popularly known as "Kidcare"—is operational and growing institutional roots in statehouses across America. Though it is well-intentioned, we foresee unintended and potentially dangerous consequences by 2020 because of Kidcare's approach to addressing children's health care needs. The root cause of a future children's health care problem will be the collapse of America's employer-provided health insurance system. We fear an expanded, government-provided Kidcare program could be disastrous once we begin this inevitable shift away from an employer-provided system. In this chapter we will describe Kidcare, and discuss what we see as its possibly onerous outcomes.

Kids lacking access to health care services is unacceptable in our society. And when our employer-provided health care system collapses, we must think creatively about ways to ensure that America's kids receive high-quality health care services.

We begin by discussing what we know about kids and what the demographics suggest might happen to children and their health care in the future.

Fifty Years Ago Babies Were Booming

In the mid-1940s America witnessed an unprecedented boom in the number of American babies. Beginning in 1946 with the return of American servicemen from World War II, American women began an unprecedented surge in childbirths that would continue at historically high levels until the mid-1960s.

Table 3.1 shows the number of children under age 18 in America over the last half-century and projected to the year 2020. In the early years of the Baby Boom generation we see a distinct jump in the number of children in America from 1950 to 1960. Children under the age of 5 catapult to close to 25 million in 1960 from just over 19 million in 1950. By the 1970s, increases in the number of young children in the population taper off, signaling the end of the Baby Boom generation.

Table 3.1 Number of children under age 18 in the United States, by age, selected years 1950-96 and projected 2000-2020 (numbers in millions).

Age	1950	1960	1970	1980	1990	1996	2000	2010	2020
All Children	47.3	64.5	69.8	63.7	64.2	69.4	70.8	72.5	77.6
Age 0-5	19.1	24.3	20.9	19.6	22.5	23.5	22.9	23.9	26.4
Age 6-11	15.3	21.8	24.6	20.8	21.6	23.2	24.3	23.6	25.8
Age 12-17	12.9	18.4	24.3	23.3	20.1	22.7	23.6	25.0	25.4

Source: U.S. Bureau of the Census Current Population Reports, Federal Interagency Forum on Child and Family Statistics, 1997.

Not surprisingly, as the massive cohort of Boomers aged they began having children themselves. By the early 1990s one sees evidence of an "echo
boom" of children of the Baby Boomers as the number of children under age 5
increased from just under 20 million in 1980 to 22.5 million by 1990. But the
"echo boom" was not nearly as dramatic as the post-World War II Baby Boom
had been. (In 1996, for example, there were fewer total children in the United
States under 18 than there had been in 1970.)

By the year 2020 the total number of children in America will reach nearly

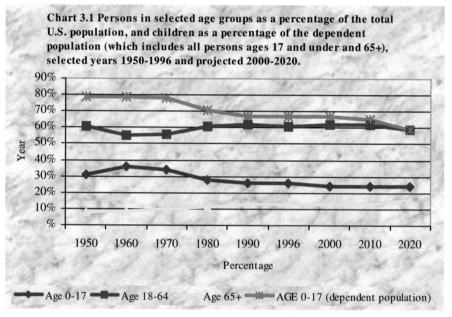

**Chart 3.1 Persons in selected age groups as a percentage of the total
U.S. population, and children as a percentage of the dependent
population (which includes all persons ages 17 and under and 65+),
selected years 1950-1996 and projected 2000-2020.**

Source: U.S. Bureau of the Census Current Population Reports, Federal Interagency
Forum on Child and Family Statistics, 1997.

78 million (see Table 3.1). Children, along with older folks, are considered
part of the "dependent" population. The dependent population, including all
persons ages 17 and under and 65 and over, is assumed to be less able to live
independently and thus considered dependent upon those aged 18-64 for many
of their needs.

In 1950, as the American Baby Boom generation began, children under
age 18 represented 31 percent of the total population (see Chart 3.1). This
percentage would climb until the early 1960s, after which the ratio of children
to others in the total population would fall to nearly one out of four.

By the turn of the century the percentage of children under the age of
18 should level off at 24 percent and remain there through 2020. But

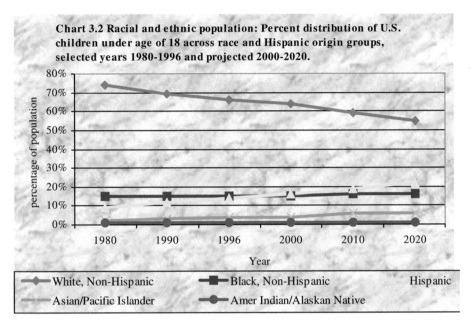

Chart 3.2 Racial and ethnic population: Percent distribution of U.S. children under age of 18 across race and Hispanic origin groups, selected years 1980-1996 and projected 2000-2020.

Source: U.S. Bureau of the Census Current Population Reports, Federal Interagency Forum on Child and Family Statistics, 1997.

America's children will represent a smaller percent of the total dependent population in coming decades, falling to 59 percent by 2020 from 79 percent in 1950. Much older Americans, as expected, will see a doubling of their percentage of the total population from a low of 8 percent in 1950 to 16 percent by 2020. (Which means Americans age 65 and over will also see their percentage of the dependent population increase.)

The race and ethnicity of tomorrow's children will be very different from today's. For example, in 1980 whites represented nearly three out of four American children. But by 2020, just forty years later, the percentage of white (non-Hispanic) children will have free-fallen to just over two out of four (see Chart 3.2).

Increasing racial and ethnic diversity among America's children is a demographic certainty. As the percentage of white American kids collapses, the percentage of certain nonwhite children will expand. Black (non-Hispanic) children will make only a modest increase in the percentage of America's children under age 18, inching up slightly from 15 percent of the population in 1980 to 16 percent by 2020. But the percentage of Hispanic and Asian/Pacific Islander children will dramatically increase. Hispanic kids will skyrocket from 9 percent of America's child population in 1980 to 22 percent by 2020. And Asian/

Pacific Islander children will also see an increase in their percentage of America's child population, jumping from 2 percent in 1980 to 6 percent by 2020.

America's children will become much more ethnically diverse in coming decades. Hispanic and Asian/Pacific Islander kids in particular will represent much higher proportions of America's child population. As the previous analysis presents, while American birth rates are not projected to change dramatically in coming decades, America's children will represent a much smaller proportion of the total American dependent population by the year 2020. This is because the massive cohort of aging Boomers will represent a rapidly rising percentage of America's dependent population by 2020.

The Health of America's Children

How healthy will America's children be in 2020? This question is perhaps best answered by first looking at the health of America's children in the past and today.

The good news is that all kids, regardless of race, ethnicity, or socioeconomic status of parents and whether they have health insurance or not, are in generally good health. As Table 3.2 presents, the percentage of American kids reported to be in very good or excellent health has hovered around 80 percent through the first part of the 1990s.

There are some troubling, though not entirely unexpected, underlying problems. Poorer kids, for example, do not report as high a percentage of children in very good or excellent health as children from wealthier backgrounds. Sixty-seven percent, or roughly two out of three children aged between 0-4 and coming from families earning less than $10,000 a year, are found to be in very good or excellent health (see Table 3.2). Comparatively, nine out of ten of kids from wealthier backgrounds (those kids whose families earn $35,000 or more a year) were reported to be in very good or excellent health in 1994.

Despite this divide in health status between kids in wealthy households versus kids in poorer households, on a host of other measures of kids' health the numbers are improving. For example, one might logically suppose that a reason for poor children's lower rates in the "very good" or "excellent" health categories would result from an inadequate diet. But the percentages of American children reported to have trouble getting enough to eat have been trending downward in recent years. As Table 3.3 reveals, in the late 1980s it was reported that 5.3 percent of all children in America were sometimes or often left with "not enough to eat." But by 1994 this percentage had been sliced by more than half, down to 2.6 percent. By

Table 3.2 Percentage of children in very good or excellent health, by age and income, 1990-1994.

Age and income	1990	1991	1992	1993	1994
Total	81	80	80	79	79
Age					
0-4 years	81	81	80	80	81
5-17 years	80	80	80	79	79
Income					
Under $10,000	62	63	65	64	63
$10,000-19,999	74	71	70	68	70
$20,000-34,999	82	82	81	88	88
$35,000 or more	89	88	89	88	88
Age and Income					
0-4 years					
Under $10,000	67	69	69	68	67
$10,000-19,999	76	74	72	72	74
$20,000-34,999	82	83	83	83	80
$35,000 or more	90	88	89	90	90
5-17 years					
Under $10,000	60	60	62	61	62
$10,000-19,999	73	70	69	67	68
$20,000-34,999	82	81	81	80	77
$35,000 or more	89	88	89	87	88

Source: Centers for Disease Control and Prevention, National Center for Health Statistics, National Health Interview Survey (1990-94), Federal Interagency Forum on Child and Family Statistics, 1997.

Table 3.3 Percent of children in America below poverty line, 1989-1994.

Poverty Level	1989	1990	1991	1994
All Children	5.3	3.8	3.5	2.6
Children in households at or below 130% of poverty	12.2	13.1	11.9	8.0
Children in households above 130% of poverty	3.0	.5	.5	.5

Source: United States Department of Agriculture Continuing Survey of Food Intakes
of Individuals, Federal Interagency Forum on Child and Family Statistics, 1997.

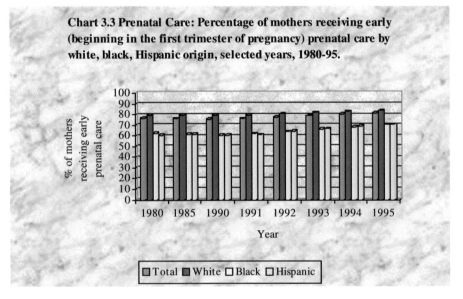

Chart 3.3 Prenatal Care: Percentage of mothers receiving early (beginning in the first trimester of pregnancy) prenatal care by white, black, Hispanic origin, selected years, 1980-95.

Source: Centers for Disease Control and Prevention, National Center for Health Statistics, National Vital Statistics System, Federal Interagency Forum on Child and Family Statistics, 1997.

1994 those children in households above 130 percent of the poverty level almost never had difficulty getting enough to eat. The percentage of these better-off kids not getting enough to eat crept close to zero. And even those children in households at or below 130 percent of the poverty level saw their percentage drop sharply from 12.2 percent of the child population in 1989 down to 8.0 percent by 1994.

There has also been a marked improvement in the percentage of American mothers receiving prenatal care during the first two trimesters of pregnancy. The Health Care Financing Administration reports that by the late 1990s almost 94 percent of all U.S. women were receiving prenatal care

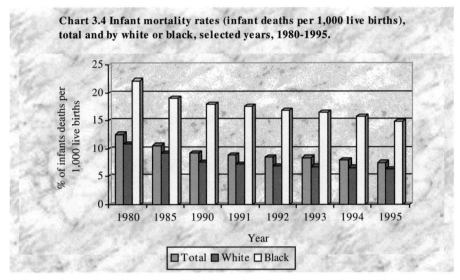

Chart 3.4 Infant mortality rates (infant deaths per 1,000 live births), total and by white or black, selected years, 1980-1995.

Source: Centers for Disease Control and Prevention, National Center for Health Statistics, National Vital Statistics System, Federal Interagency Forum on Child and Family Statistics, 1997.

within these first two trimesters, with only 6 percent waiting until the third trimester or getting no care at all.

During the first critical trimester of development the percentage of American women getting prenatal care has seen an upswing in just the last twenty years. The percentage of all women receiving prenatal care moved up from 76.3 percent in 1980 to over 80 percent by 1995. Black women and women of Hispanic origin increased their percentage of women receiving early prenatal care. Black women receiving care during the first trimester of pregnancy jumped from 62.4 percent in 1980 to 70.3 percent in 1995. And women of Hispanic origin receiving early prenatal care vaulted up from just over 60 percent in 1980 to over 70 percent by 1995 (see Chart 3.3).

Infant and Child Mortality Rates

In America in recent years infant and child mortality rates have been reduced. Total infant mortality rates (infant deaths per 1,000 live births) were cut almost in half from 1980 to 1995 (see Chart 3.4). White infant mortality rates dropped from just under eleven deaths per 1,000 live births in 1980 to just over six in 1995 and black infant mortality rates dropped from 22.2 deaths per 1,000 live births in 1980 to under fifteen by 1995.

Child mortality rates also declined sharply from the early 1980s to the mid-1990s. Mortality rates for all children between ages 1 and 4 fell from

Table 3.4 Child mortality rates (deaths per 100,000 resident population in each age group), by age, race and Hispanic origin, selected years 1980-94.

Characteristic	1980	1985	1990	1991	1992	1993	1994
Ages 1-4							
Total	63.9	51.8	46.8	47.4	43.6	44.8	42.9
Male	72.6	58.5	52.4	52.0	48.0	49.5	47.3
Female	54.7	44.8	41.0	42.7	39.0	39.9	38.2
White	57.9	46.6	41.1	41.7	38.1	38.4	36.5
Black	97.6	80.7	76.8	79.7	73.2	79.1	77.2
Asian/Pacific Islander	43.2	40.1	38.6	30.4	26.9	30.5	25.3
Hispanic	——	48.2	48.1	47.7	41.7	42.0	39.1
Characteristic	**1980**	**1985**	**1990**	**1991**	**1992**	**1993**	**1994**
Ages 5-14							
Total	30.6	26.5	24.0	23.6	22.5	23.4	22.5
Male	36.7	31.8	28.5	28.7	27.2	27.4	26.9
Female	24.7	21.0	19.3	18.3	17.5	19.1	17.9
White	29.1	24.9	22.3	22.0	20.6	21.4	20.3
Black	39.0	35.5	34.4	34.2	33.7	35.1	34.8
Asian/Pacific Islander	22.5	20.8	16.9	15.1	16.1	17.1	16.2
Hispanic	——	19.6	21.7	21.5	21.0	22.6	20.1

—— = data not available

Source: Centers for Disease Control and Prevention, National Center for Health Statistics, National Vital Statistics System, Federal Interagency Forum on Child and Family Statistics, 1997.

almost sixty-four deaths per 100,000 resident population in 1980 to under forty-three deaths per resident population by 1994 (see Table 3.4). And black mortality rates for very young children fell considerably, from just under 100 per 100,000 resident population in 1980 to just over seventy-seven by 1994.

Table 3.5 Percentage of low-birthweight births (<2500 grams or approximately 5.5 lbs.), total and by white, black or Hispanic origin, selected years 1980-95.

Race & Hispanic origin	1980	1985	1990	1991	1992	1993	1994	1995
Total	6.8	6.8	7.0	7.1	7.1	7.2	7.3	7.3
White	5.7	5.7	5.7	5.8	5.8	6.0	6.1	6.2
Black	12.7	12.7	13.3	13.6	13.3	13.3	13.2	13.0
Hispanic origin	6.1	6.2	6.1	6.2	6.1	6.2	6.3	6.3

Source: Centers for Disease Control and Prevention, National Center for Health Statistics, National Vital Statistics System, Federal Interagency Forum on Child and Family Statistics, 1997.

On a host of variables—percentages of children without enough to eat, of children receiving prenatal care, and of infant and child mortality rates—there are encouraging signs that children's health care has been improving. However, one statistic regarding childrens' health care in America is troubling: the percentage of low-birthweight births has been trending upwards in recent years. As Table 3.5 reveals, over the fifteen-year period between 1980 and 1995 the percent of low-birthweight births increased for all women—whites, blacks, and women of Hispanic origin included.

Table 3.5 is alarming. Why, when so many other variables regarding children's health are improving, do we see the percentage of low-birthweight births increasing? For clues, consider an earlier rise in teen birth rates or the rise in birth rates for unmarried women over the past twenty years. Teenagers and unmarried women face an enormous struggle in caring for the basic needs of young children. One might logically assume that teenagers—and particularly unmarried teenagers—would have more difficulty in accessing health care coverage for an expanding family.

Table 3.6 reveals teen birth rates (births per 1,000 females) by age, race, and Hispanic origin from 1980 to 1994. While teen birth rates for whites and American Indian/Alaskan Native women did not greatly move up or down over this fifteen-year period, rates for blacks, Asian/Pacific Islander, and Hispanic women increased considerably.

Table 3.7 shows birth rates for unmarried women by age of the mother from 1980 to 1994. These rates (births per 1,000 unmarried women) jumped from below thirty in 1980 to almost forty-seven by 1994. For all age cohorts—from ages 15-17 up to 40-44—the birth rates for American unmarried women climbed steadily during the 1980s and continued into the 1990s.

Table 3.6 Teen birth rates (births per 1,000 females in each age group) by age, race, and Hispanic origin), selected years 1980-94.

Age All races	1980	1985	1990	1991	1992	1993	1994
10-14 years	1.1	1.2	1.4	1.4	1.4	1.4	1.4
15-17 years	32.5	31.0	37.5	38.7	37.8	37.8	37.6
18-19 years	82.1	79.6	88.6	94.4	94.5	92.1	91.5
White, non-Hispanic	**1980**	**1985**	**1990**	**1991**	**1992**	**1993**	**1994**
10-14 years	0.4	——	0.5	0.5	0.5	0.5	0.5
15-17 years	22.4	——	23.2	23.6	22.7	22.7	22.8
18-19 years	67.7	——	66.6	70.5	69.8	67.7	67.4
Black	**1980**	**1985**	**1990**	**1991**	**1992**	**1993**	**1994**
10-14 years	4.3	4.5	4.9	4.8	4.7	4.6	4.6
15-17 years	72.5	69.3	82.3	84.1	81.3	79.8	76.3
18-19 years	135.1	132.4	152.9	158.6	157.9	151.9	148.3
Asian/Pacific Islander	**1980**	**1985**	**1990**	**1991**	**1992**	**1993**	**1994**
10-14 years	0.3	0.4	0.7	0.8	0.7	0.6	0.7
15-17 years	12.0	12.5	16.0	16.1	15.2	16.0	16.1
18-19 years	46.2	40.8	40.2	43.1	43.1	43.3	44.1
Hispanic	**1980**	**1985**	**1990**	**1991**	**1992**	**1993**	**1994**
10-14 years	1.7	——	2.4	2.4	2.6	2.7	2.7
15-17 years	52.1	——	65.9	70.6	71.4	71.7	74.0
18-19 years	82.2	——	100.3	106.7	107.1	106.8	107.7
Amer. Indian/Alaskan Native							
10-14 years	1.9	1.7	1.6	1.6	1.6	1.4	1.9
15-17 years	51.5	47.7	48.5	52.7	53.8	53.7	51.3
18-19 years	129.5	124.1	129.3	134.3	132.6	130.7	130.3

——= data not available

Source: Centers for Disease Control and Prevention, National Center for Health Statistics, National Vital Statistics System, Federal Interagency Forum on Child and Family Statistics, 1997.

Children's Health Care Insurance

The percentage of health care insurance from all public and private sources for America's children has remained steady from the late 1980s on into the mid-1990s. As Table 3.8 reveals, child health insurance rates did not budge appreciably up or down from 87 percent of all children during this almost ten-year cycle. And the percentage of black children covered by health insurance has actually seen a slight upsurge.

But this composite score of total child health care insurance masks important changes going on within the health care insurance market for kids. Consider Table 3.9 which reveals the percentage of children under 18 covered by *private* health insurance by age, race, and Hispanic origin during this same cycle of years. All children—the very youngest and the oldest, and across race and Hispanic origin—have experienced a falling off in

Table 3.7 Birth Rates for unmarried women (births per 1,000 unmarried women) by age of mother, 1980-94.

Year	Total (15-44)	15-17	18-19	20-24	25-29	30-34	35-39	40-44
1980	29.4	20.6	39.0	40.9	34.0	21.1	9.7	2.6
1981	29.5	20.9	39.0	41.1	34.5	20.8	9.8	2.6
1982	30.0	21.5	39.6	41.5	35.1	21.9	10.0	2.7
1983	30.3	22.0	40.7	41.8	35.5	22.4	10.2	2.6
1984	31.0	21.9	42.5	43.0	37.1	23.3	10.9	2.5
1985	32.8	22.4	45.9	46.5	39.9	25.2	11.6	2.5
1986	34.2	22.8	48.0	49.3	42.2	27.2	12.2	2.7
1987	36.0	24.5	48.9	52.6	44.5	29.6	13.5	2.9
1988	38.5	26.4	51.5	56.0	48.5	32.0	15.0	3.2
1989	41.6	28.7	56.0	61.2	52.8	34.9	16.0	3.4
1990	43.8	29.6	60.7	65.1	56.0	37.6	17.3	3.6
1991	45.2	30.9	65.7	68.0	56.5	38.1	18.0	3.8
1992	45.2	30.4	67.3	68.5	56.5	37.9	18.8	4.1
1993	45.3	30.6	66.9	69.2	57.1	38.5	19.0	4.4
1994	46.9	32.0	70.1	72.2	59.0	40.1	19.8	4.7

Source: Centers for Disease Control and Prevention, National Center for Health Statistics, National Vital Statistics System, Advance Report of Final Natality Statistics, Federal Interagency Forum on Child and Family Statistics, 1997.

their percentage of private health insurance coverage from the late 1980s to the mid-1990s. This is not unexpected, as increasing downsizing by large companies, an upsurge in temporary employment, and health care price inflation have caused more employers to alter their private health care coverage options for their employees.

So why has there been an overall increase in health care insurance coverage for children? Since the late 1980s *public* health care programs have been signing up increasing numbers of children (see Table 3.10), replacing the coverage previously provided by private health care insurance.

Medicaid and the Origins of Kidcare

More than thirty years after its introduction, the federal Medicaid program is today one of the most expensive and fastest-growing of America's entitlement programs. Designed to provide health care for poor and

Table 3.8 Total health insurance: Percentage of children under age 18 covered by public and private health insurance by age, race, and Hispanic origin, 1987-95.

	1987	1988	1989	1990	1991	1992	1993	1994	1995
All Children	87	87	87	87	87	87	86	86	86
Age 0-5	88	87	89	89	89	89	88	86	87
Age 6-11	87	87	87	87	88	88	87	87	87
Age 12-17	86	86	86	85	85	85	83	85	86
Race and Hispanic origin									
White	88	88	88	87	88	88	87	87	87
Black	83	84	84	85	85	86	84	83	85
Hispanic	72	71	70	72	73	75	74	72	73

Source: U.S. Bureau of the Census, Housing and Household Economic Statistics Division, Federal Interagency Forum on Child and Family Statistics, 1997.

underserved populations, Medicaid (along with its counterpart Medicare, the comprehensive health insurance program for senior citizens) was enacted as part of the 1965 Social Security Amendments to address what lawmakers viewed as deficient health care services for the nation's poor.

In a classic case of unintended consequences, policymakers in the 1960s expected Medicaid costs to begin and remain only a small fraction of government expenditures. But from a relatively meager $1.3 billion ($600 million from the federal government and $700 million from states) in its opening year, Medicaid would quickly gobble up larger and larger percentages of government spending. By the late 1980s Medicaid would top $50 billion in combined federal and state spending, and by 1995 total spending would spike up to almost $160 billion.

The primary cause of this explosion in Medicaid spending has been an expansion of federal and state eligibility requirements. Medicaid today is actually a combination of four different programs: health insurance for welfare recipients, medical care for pregnant women and young children slightly above the poverty level, long-term medical and custodial care for disabled Americans, and long-term medical and custodial care for the elderly.

But in the late 1990s the federal government noticed a breakdown in the Medicaid system. There was no government-provided health insurance to cover the kids of parents who either made too much money for Medicaid, did not get family insurance through their job, or made lifestyle choices

Table 3.9 Health Insurance coverage: Percentage of children under age 18 covered by private health insurance by age, race, and Hispanic origin, 1987-1995.

	1987	1988	1989	1990	1991	1992	1993	1994	1995
All Children	74	74	74	71	70	69	67	66	66
Age 0-5	72	71	71	68	66	65	63	60	60
Age 6-11	74	74	75	73	71	71	70	67	67
Age 12-17	75	76	76	73	72	71	69	70	71
Race and Hispanic origin									
White	79	79	78	76	75	74	72	71	71
Black	49	50	52	49	45	46	46	43	44
Hispanic	48	48	48	45	43	42	42	38	38

Source: U.S. Bureau of the Census, Housing and Household Economic Statistics Division, Federal Interagency Forum on Child and Family Statistics, 1997.

that excluded their kids from health insurance.

So, in the late 1990s well-intentioned health care policy experts and government planners pushed for and later enacted sweeping legislation to provide insurance for these kids. Popularly known as "Kidcare," this legislation was intended to shore up Medicaid's failures in getting health insurance for poor children.

The supporters of Kidcare delivered a highly sophisticated political message that pitted the good guys (those in favor of this particular legislative version of Kidcare) against the bad guys (those in favor of any alternative plan).

But while this debate over Kidcare was arguably intellectually dishonest, it was also clearly politically persuasive. The "feel-good" phraseology of the term "Kidcare" caused most politicians to jump on board the legislation out of fear of being branded hostile to kids' health care.

By the time the political dust had settled, those in favor of an ambitious federal/state program to address apparent inadequacies in children's health care coverage were victorious. As part of the Balanced Budget Act of 1997 the U.S. Congress passed, and President Clinton signed, the State Children's Health Insurance Program (S-CHIP).

S-CHIP, now commonly known as Kidcare, provides federal matching funds directly to states to assist in provisioning child health care assistance to uninsured, low-income children. A part of the Balanced Budget

Act of 1997, S-CHIP appropriates funds for each of the fiscal years 1998 through 2007.

Children's Health Care Coverage in the Future: What Should We Do?

We believe the focus of children's health care in coming decades should be on improving kids' access to health care services, and not necessarily extending government health care insurance to uninsured kids. When the Baby Boomers begin their massive march out of the American workforce early in the twenty-first century, our employer-provided health insurance will be forever changed. Some will look to expanding government-provided health insurance programs such as Medicaid, Kidcare, and Medicare to fill the vacuum of citizens knocked out of the employer-provided market.

But as we argued in Chapter 2, these government-provided health care programs will sink under the weight of their promises. There simply are not enough non-Boomer workers to support the retired Boomers. Which means the costs of supporting federal health care programs including Kidcare—may become so confiscatory as to court open rebellion among working Americans.

Our reading of current trends suggests that America will continue shifting away from our historically bizarre employer-provided system. As this fundamental transformation accelerates in the early part of the twenty-first century, policymakers will be confronted with unprecedented health policy challenges.

One of the biggest hurdles policymakers will face in coming years will be making health care services *easier* for parents and children to access by improving parents' *knowledge* of available health care services. The U.S. General Accounting Office already acknowledges that there have been consistent failures in signing eligible children up for existing Medicaid programs: in 1994, for instance, almost 3 million uninsured children met Medicaid guidelines for eligibility and yet were not enrolled in this federal-state program. In a recent study of a major American medical device company less than half of the 2-year-old children of employees were current in their required immunizations. The reasons for this low immunization record? A detailed analysis blames a lack of convenience and a lack of knowledge on the part of the parents.

Policy Prescriptions for Dealing with Children's Health Care Needs

In the near term, we believe there are three sets of measures that could be taken to improve children's access to health care services.

Table 3.10 Health Insurance coverage: Percentage of children under age 18 covered by public health insurance by age, race, and Hispanic origin, 1987-1995.

	1987	1988	1989	1990	1991	1992	1993	1994	1995
All children	19	19	19	22	24	25	27	26	26
Age 0-5	22	23	24	28	30	33	35	33	33
Age 6-11	19	18	18	20	22	23	25	25	26
Age 12-17	16	16	15	18	19	19	20	20	21
Race and Hispanic origin									
White	14	14	15	17	19	20	22	21	21
Black	42	42	41	45	48	49	50	48	49
Hispanic	28	27	27	32	37	38	41	38	39

Source: U.S. Bureau of the Census, Housing and Household Economic Statistics Division, Federal Interagency Forum on Child and Family Statistics, 1997.

Short-term Option 1: Welfare Reform as the Vehicle for Increasing Health Insurance Coverage

Cries to reform "welfare-as-we-know-it" raise the question of what is to be the fate of persons currently covered by Medicaid if such policies are carried forth. Could the nation wind up with even more uninsured persons? How do we go about establishing a low-income health assistance program not tied to welfare? This is a "defensive" question. In the short run, how do we avoid things getting worse as current welfare recipients become employed and Medicaid-ineligible? It is short run in the sense that this debate has already been engaged. But the welfare debate also opens opportunities for "offense" through extending health insurance subsidies to low-income working families, a population with a high incidence of uninsurance.

And if we expect to have any chance of caring for the Boomers in their dotage, there cannot be many unproductive, working-age citizens.

The challenge of expanding health care services and insurance coverage easily draws us into overall questions of health care policy and even tax policy reform. Because of this, attempts to improve significantly the way we help low-income families access and afford health coverage have so far tended to collapse with the failure to establish consensus on broader systemic reforms.

But this need not be the case. It is currently within the realm of possibility to reform and improve substantially the way health care assistance is provided to low-income families and children as part of the welfare reform discussion.

States across the nation are beginning to review critically how well, and how poorly, their various systems of public aid serve low-income families and children. The movement to reform cash welfare has been at the center of these efforts, but it is important to consider how health care policy can—and is—being affected by these welfare reform efforts. Reforming the way we help poor families find and afford health coverage is an integral part of what needs to be done to improve public assistance generally. There is an opportunity to take important steps to improve coverage for low-income families within the context of broader welfare changes.

Indeed, it is fair to say that where broader health care policy reform efforts have failed to resolve the coverage problems faced by many low-income families, the public's interest in welfare reform has rekindled the attention policymakers must pay to how poor families are helped to meet health care needs, especially when they are expected to enter and sustain themselves in the workforce. Welfare reform can be the horse to ride in the short run. Welfare reform forces the political system to deal with the question of health coverage for low-income families and children generally. And if we do not face this question, the Boomer retirement problem becomes intractable. There are not enough resources to go around.

We recommend pursuing a pragmatic approach to expanding and rationalizing health insurance coverage by aggressively engaging in the broader reform debates taking place nationally (and more importantly in statehouses), presenting solutions that help meet the needs of families and children who are not covered, and doing so in a way that improves their prospects of escaping welfare and becoming economically self-sufficient.

Medicaid's Limitations

Through Medicaid, national and state governments spend hundreds of billions of dollars annually to provide health care coverage for low-income families. Over the past decade, Medicaid coverage of low-income persons has been expanded considerably.

Yet, as a program intended to help the poor obtain health care services, and as part of a broader public assistance system in each state, the current Medicaid program has serious drawbacks. Medicaid has become the single most expensive part of a Byzantine system of welfare-oriented programs operated by the states. Its evolving legislative history has resulted in complex eligibility rules and a program that provides coverage only to select portions of the poor.

Among families with dependent children, Medicaid has traditionally been available to those families who receive welfare. Herein lies the central issue that engages medical assistance in the debate over welfare reform. Among the most important barriers families face when leaving welfare is the loss of health care coverage. Over the past decade, a number of federal and state policy changes have been made attempting to ameliorate this problem—by extending the period of time a family remains eligible for Medicaid while "transitioning" off welfare, and by expanding Medicaid coverage to select populations of (mostly) children based upon income and not upon their connection to welfare programs. Kidcare is the latest of these attempts.

Despite this, families who leave welfare must still face the reality that Medicaid coverage will at some time end.

The type of coverage Medicaid provides is also distinctly different from health care insurance generally available to many families through their employers. Medicaid covers many services that are not typically covered in private plans, and does not require the significant coinsurance or copays often required by plans available (if any) to those who leave welfare. This has become even more the case as private coverage has declined in recent years.

Use of MSAs in Welfare Reform

We recommend pursuing reforms at the state level with other strategies designed to promote upward mobility and self-sufficiency of poor families.

1) Convert Medicaid for welfare recipients into low-income health assistance.

We recommend states carve out the portion of their Medicaid programs that finance normal family health care coverage (i.e., exclude long-term care) for welfare recipients and other covered children and individuals. Use those funds to establish a broadly based health care assistance program for low-income families. Eligibility should be open to all disabled parents (who do not have other coverage options) with dependent children and all able-bodied parents who are working, or who are pursuing work in accordance with the policies of the state's public assistance system.

This program must extend to all low-income families, not just to former welfare recipients. If limited only to former welfare recipients, two highly undesirable consequences would follow. First, it would create a perverse incentive for the working poor to cycle into welfare just so cycling out would provide an insurance subsidy. Second, those working poor choosing not to do this (and perhaps with no health insurance themselves) would feel an intense antipathy toward former welfare recipients. A co-worker with the same income would be better off for once having been on welfare. This is not the way to social harmony.

Medical Savings Accounts are particularly well-suited for such a program.

MSAs—A "Soft Way" to Apply "Tough Love"

MSAs are a way to return health care buying power to the consumer, the patient, and the patient's doctor. They short-circuit government entitlement programs, HMOs, and other insurance company third-party payments.

Under an MSA, "someone" purchases a high-deductible health insurance policy. We suggest in Chapter 2 that this may well be through repeal of the tax exclusion for employment-based health insurance, and replacement by a universal tax credit for purchase of high-deductible insurance. "High-deductible" simply means that the first X thousand of health insurance outlays are paid for by the individual. A $3000 deductible is an often-mentioned figure. Above $3,000 the insurance policy kicks in and the policy pays for medical expenses in excess of that amount.

What about smaller expenses? A "Medical Savings Account" is established—perhaps amounting to one or two thousand dollars—to take care of smaller medical bills. If the MSA money is not spent on medical care in the year it is available, it may either be withdrawn and spent on other things, or rolled over to the next year to help take care of future medical expenses. The MSA could be funded either by conversion of present medical entitlements—Medicaid, for example—or by private firms that still retain an interest in health care coverage for their employees. The maximum liability for an individual or family is the difference between the MSA contribution and the amount of the insurance policy deductible.

MSAs are a "soft way" to apply "tough love"—teaching not just money management but personal responsibility. A former welfare recipient engaged in "Medicaid" behavior (as most of us would do if someone else were paying the bills) would quickly learn this behavior has adverse personal consequences. The bill for the horror story case of calling an ambulance to go to the emergency room for treatment for a cold would be paid, but paid from the MSA, leaving the individual at the end of the year with less MSA money than would otherwise be his. Further, MSAs act in effect as a medical trust account. Unlike cash assistance, MSA funds cannot be converted to socially undesirable purchases such as illegal drugs. Former welfare recipients would rapidly come to understand that wise use of their MSA funds would make funds available at the end of the year for other uses they may value highly, such as better housing or education.

The design of such a plan is simple in concept but would vary in detail depending on each state's level of Medicaid benefits and current Medicaid population (and therefore the pool of money made available), and the number of working poor. Based upon these calculations, the authorities would determine the size of the deductible on the insurance they would purchase for each family and individual in the program. This could be a single statewide purchase. The gap between the deductible on the catastrophic policy and the amount of the MSA deposit would be very small for the lowest earners, with the MSA deposit gradually phasing out as the family or individual income increases. The phaseout schedule would be determined by available resources. To avoid a "cliff" of catastrophic insurance "switching off" with the next dollar of income beyond the income level where the MSA deposit is zero, the deductible on the catastrophic insurance could be phased upward as earnings rise. At some income level, the deductible would be so high as to effectively be no insurance at all.

Some former welfare recipients will become employed in jobs with insurance coverage, and some current low-income working households are also employed in jobs with health insurance. In those cases, offer them a choice of their employer's insurance or the MSA. If they choose the MSA, the employer should be required to make a contribution to the low-income medical assistance fund for having been relieved of the burden of insuring that person and family.

If we believe able-bodied parents can be expected to support themselves, and that public assistance should be oriented toward helping them do just that, then it makes far greater sense for medical assistance to be constructed as a low-income worker support program. Health care can become part of creating better opportunities for families and children, rather than becoming a barrier.

The differential tax treatment of employer-provided versus individually acquired health insurance is going to break down, either because current MSA supporters carry the day, or later when the tax exclusion for employer-provided insurance is repealed. At either point, we believe MSAs will become much more prevalent in the general population. Why not let the poorest among us be the wave of the future?

2) Pay close attention to effective marginal tax rates.

Health care is but one of a number of subsidies based on income available to low-income families. Moving up the income ladder means giving up public benefits. In certain income ranges, the combined benefits loss under current programs can be over 100 percent—a crushing marginal tax rate. Many welfare families cannot "afford" to take a job.

In designing a low-income health insurance assistance program based on MSAs (or crafted any other way), attention should be given to imposing the smallest feasible implicit marginal tax rate so as to minimize the disincentive to earn more. What this amounts to will vary with the circumstances of each individual state and the resources available from former Medicaid funds. It may not be possible in all states to avoid steep implicit marginal tax rates, but they should be minimized to the extent possible in crafting the plan.

There is some reason to believe that very high implicit marginal tax rates can be avoided in many, if not most, cases. First, states with small Medicaid populations and correspondingly small amounts of Medicaid money are also typically states with relatively small numbers of working poor. Conversely, states with large numbers of working poor also tend to be states with large Medicaid populations. High demand for the new program also tends to be matched by high resource availability, and vice versa.

Second, much of the Medicaid population is young. The working poor are also mostly young. Catastrophic insurance for the young is very cheap. Medicaid is "Cadillac" coverage that can be overutilized. It is expensive, and very large amounts of money will become available to any low-income health assistance program. Our own back-of-the-envelope calculation, based on Indiana numbers, is that a low-income MSA program might only impose an implicit marginal tax rate of 20 percent. This will obviously vary by state, but Indiana is likely fairly typical.

Short-term Option 2: Unemployment Compensation: COBRA Counseling

In theory, no employee with employer-provided health insurance need be without insurance for the first year of unemployment. By paying 102 percent of the prior premium, COBRA coverage may be maintained, and the employee (and children) will continue health insurance coverage. "COBRA" is an acronym for the Comprehensive Budget Reconciliation Act—a federal law which mandates employers to continue a former employee's employment-based health insurance for a limited period of time if the employee pays the premium.

In practice, this is simply not the case. We individually interviewed twenty-six small business firms at a meeting of the Indiana Chamber of Commerce Small Business Council. Nearly half said they did not routinely inform employees who were leaving of COBRA rights. (All would deny this publicly.) We believe this to be a widespread practice, especially for employees known to have an expensive medical condition (e.g., pregnancy). Administrators of the Indiana State Unemployment Compensation (UC) program inform us that there is no systematic program to inform the unemployed of COBRA rights when applying for UC. A check with two other Midwestern state UC programs yielded the same answer. There are recently unemployed who would have continued health insurance but do not because of ignorance about CO-BRA rights. Either the employee cannot afford the premium difference for the more expensive private insurance (but would have continued under COBRA), or the employee is so conditioned to think of insurance as being employment-based that he is unaware that there are other insurance alternatives.

A very simple and cheap strategy to increase health insurance coverage for children would be to induce state UC administrators to make certain their staff inform recently unemployed clients of their COBRA rights

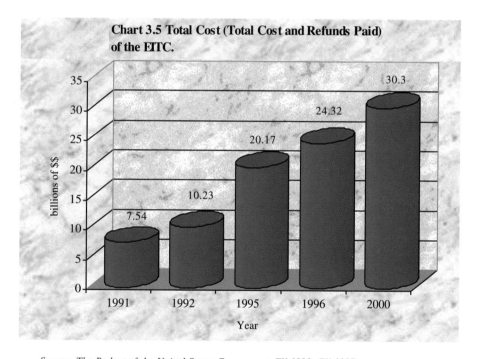

Source: The Budget of the United States Government, FY 1993; FY 1997.

at the time they first file for UC.

A public policy foundation or other nongovernmental organization interested in improving children's health care coverage could facilitate this by a variety of means. The "brute force" method would be to host a one-day conference for all fifty UC chiefs, urging them to implement a COBRA rights information policy. A more cost-effective approach might be to prepare a one-page COBRA information sheet. A foundation or other nongovernmental organization might announce the availability of a small "planning" grant, perhaps $1,000, to each state UC department willing to implement the policy of including the information sheet with every new client's filing.

We cannot precisely quantify what effect such an action might have on the availability of health insurance for children. We do believe it will have some positive, immediate impact at very modest cost.

Short-term Option 3: Using the Earned Income Tax Credit to Increase Health Care Coverage

The Earned Income Tax Credit (EITC) has been little noticed as a potential tool to increase health insurance coverage. We consider here how the EITC, already targeted to families with children, could be used in the short run to increase health insurance coverage among American children. There are administrative complexities to be overcome in this option, but we lay it out as a possibility.

Growth in the magnitude of the generosity of the EITC has not been sufficiently appreciated in health policy discussions. From a program that began in the mid-70s as a device to undo the regressivity of the payroll tax for Social Security and Medicare for low-income earners, the EITC has evolved into a large transfer program that writes some families checks for more than $3,500 per year (see Chart 3.5).

This chapter has already discussed moving Medicaid to a generalized MSA-based low-income health assistance program. Such a program moves eligibility from a "cliff" where $1 additional income makes one ineligible for assistance to a "slope" creating a broader range over which subsidies would be available. Such a change would make Medicaid more like the Earned Income Tax Credit. Just as making Medicaid more like the EITC could increase the number eligible for public subsidies for health coverage, so could restructuring the EITC to make it fit better with buying health insurance.

What Is the EITC and How Does It Work?

The EITC is a federal income tax credit available to low-income working persons. As its name suggests, the amount of the credit is tied to earnings (not to income: neither unearned income [such as interest] or transfers [such as public assistance payments] are included).

For example, a parent with one child who works year round at the minimum wage of $5.15 an hour would have a monthly earned income of $885.80.

Table 3.11 Comparison of Medicaid and EITC Eligibility

	Medicaid	EITC
Extent of eligibility	*Binary: you are or you are not*	*Scaled: Extent of credit depends on income*
Personal characteristics that determine eligibility	*Income, assets, family characteristics (single parent household), disability.)*	*Income, number of children.*
Administration	*Welfare system*	*Income tax system*

(Including Food Stamps that parent would have a monthly earned income of $1,011.80.) Adding the federal EITC of $2,271.00 to this parent's income bumps the gross annual income (including earned wages, Food Stamps, and the federal EITC) to $14,412.60. A parent with two children earning the minimum hourly wage of $5.15 an hour would be eligible for a federal EITC of $3,756.00, adding to a gross annual income (including Food Stamps) of $17,061.60.

Unlike current Medicaid and its "cliff," the EITC has a "slope." The value of the EITC gradually decreases as income rises. For example, consider again the parent with one child referred to above. If this person's hourly wage increased from $5.15 an hour to $7.00 an hour, the federal EITC would drop from $2,271.00 to $1,917.00. (Note, however, that this person's gross annual income would increase from $14,412.60 to $16,365.00.) The parent with two children whose hourly wage rises from $5.15 an hour to $7.00 an hour would find her gross annual income increase from $17,061.60 to $19,502.00.

Credit-eligible individuals have two choices for the way and the frequency with which they receive the credit. The first is as part of the tax return filing process. For these recipients, the credit has the appearance of an income tax refund, coming as a once-a-year check that arrives after they file their income tax returns. The second is the advance payment option. This option allows individuals to receive the credit as part of their regular paychecks, acting as "reverse withholding;" rather than withholding an amount for federal income taxes, an individual receives an additional amount in her or his paycheck.

While advance payment would allow EITC recipients to increase their consumption equally throughout the year, advance payment has not proven popular. Over 90 percent of EITC recipients receive the credit on a lump sum, once-a-year basis. Reluctance to take advantage of the advance payment option appears to stem from three sources. The first is a reluctance by EITC recipients to further involve their employers in their personal lives. Advance payment would tell employers more about employees' living circumstances. The second is a reluctance to let go of the lump sum. Low-income families appear to view the EITC payment as a quick booster shot to their incomes; for some, it is an opportunity to catch up or get ahead on paying bills. For others, it is a windfall that can be used to purchase goods and services not affordable within their "normal" incomes. The third, and perhaps most important, is a fear of doing something that would lead to getting into trouble with the Internal Revenue Service. One source of fear relates to a perceived potential obligation to repay money to the IRS if the family somehow lost eligibility for the EITC and needed to repay the amount. The second source of fear relates to the complexity of the tax system; some low-income families, with no complexity to their tax returns, nonetheless use tax preparers.

The EITC Liquidity Constraints and Lack of Health Insurance

The EITC opens up the potential to address an insufficiently appreciated source of lack of health insurance: liquidity constraints. Neoclassical economic theory suggests that consumers smooth consumption through time; the assumption that individuals can freely borrow and lend across time periods makes the theory plausible. Thus individuals who have high incomes in one year and low (or even negative) incomes in another experience far less variation in their consumption patterns than in their income patterns. Economist Milton Friedman called this "permanent income." A standard example is farm families: while crop prices and crop yields may cause annual income to move erratically from one year to the next, farm families' spending on shelter, food, and clothing varies far less from year to year.

The "borrow-and-lend" assumption suggests two sources of lendable funds that a family expecting an EITC payment might turn to for funds to pay its health insurance premium. The first is the family's own savings; the second is the capital market (banks, etc.)

Turning to individual funds is very unlikely. One of the most frequently made points about the uninsured is that they have lower incomes than the average American. Another is that the uninsured are younger than average. Little noticed thus far has been that the uninsured have fewer assets than the insured, even at the same income and age levels.

As Table 3.12 shows, more than half of uninsured families ("median" means half are above and half are below) with incomes below $15,000 do not have a single dollar of financial assets (i.e., checking account balances, savings accounts, money market accounts, stocks, bonds, Individual Retirement Accounts, etc.) Even in the $15,000 - $30,000 range, a level that includes all EITC recipients, more than half of the uninsured families appear to have less than $300 in assets. If it is unlikely that EITC recipients could "borrow and lend" against their future lump sum EITC payments using their own savings, could they go to outside sources?

Overcoming the Liquidity Constraint

This section outlines two approaches to making the EITC more usable as a means to pay for private health insurance. The first is to use private credit markets. The second is to make the EITC a transferable credit. If EITC recipients want to buy health insurance, these steps will make it easier for them to do so.

Table 3.12 Median Financial Assets, by Current Household Income (1989 dollars).

	Below $15,000		$15,000 - $30,000	
	Insured	Uninsured	Insured	Uninsured
All households	$1,000	0	$4,100	360
Age of family head:				
Below 35	670	0	2,300	275
35 - 44	5,000	0	4,100	200
45 - 54	1,325	0	6,320	2,000
55 - 64	1,000	6	11,900	300
number	(165)	(192)	(335)	(58)

Source: Tabulations from the Survey of Consumer Finances, in Martha Starr-McCluer, "Health Insurance and Precautionary. Savings," American Economic Review 86 (1996) 289.

Private credit markets. If credit markets were willing to accept the potential of a future lump sum EITC payment as collateral, the "borrow-and-lend" constraint could be overcome. If used as part of a strategy to increase health insurance coverage, offerers of health coverage, either on their own or through credit-originating institutions (e.g., banks), could in effect accept the EITC as payment towards health coverage for children. Such loans would resemble, in form, refund anticipation loans that currently allow EITC recipients to receive their lump sum at the time they file rather than at the time the Internal Revenue Service mails a check.

Absent the cooperation of the Internal Revenue Service or state employment services in making past earnings records available, this credit would be high-risk. In the presence of such risk, credit would be high-cost, meaning that individuals who wanted to use their EITC to purchase health insurance would be required to accept a high discount rate from their EITC or, seen from the other direction, a high premium to their insurance cost. Such risk might be so high that private credit markets might not be willing to provide the credit.

Transaction costs and credit risk would be less for individuals who used their EITC to supplement the publicly provided insurance subsidy that would replace Medicaid, a step discussed earlier. The process of applying for the public subsidy would verify income, providing a higher degree of confidence to any potential lender about the level of risk involved. By combining the EITC and the public subsidy, more people would have enough resources to pay for health insurance without dipping into current earnings.

Transferable credit. Under this option, EITC recipients could pay for health insurance for themselves and their children by transferring their EITC to a health insurer. By "signing over" some or all of the expected EITC to a provider of health coverage, an individual could apply his or her EITC to health insurance without tapping credit markets.

Transfers would be mediated through the organization that oversees the EITC, IRS. However, the administration of the transferred credit need not involve interaction between individuals and the IRS. The administration of the credit would be invisible to individuals. Individuals who wanted to use their EITC to purchase health insurance would indicate that desire to the insurer; the insurer would query the IRS (much as lenders offering refund anticipation loans do) about the eligibility of the individual for the EITC; the IRS would notify the insurer of the likely credit amount; and the insurer would then apply the value of the credit towards the cost of health insurance. Some families—for example, a single parent, two-child family, with income just too high for the children to qualify for Medicaid's "poor kids" coverage—would, in most markets, have a sufficient credit amount to pay for their health insurance coverage for a year.

Fraud and financial soundness concerns could be addressed through several devices: 1) not all the expected credit could be transferable; 2) insurers would receive a payment of less than the full amount of the transfer, with the discount covering cases where the actual credit amount turns out to be less than the expected credit; 3) prior approval of the transfer by the IRS would be limited to cases where it was likely that the individual would receive a credit (i.e., based on statistical models and extrapolating from previous years' tax returns). Organizations to which the credit was transferred (health insurers, HMOs, etc.) would realize the credit in one of two ways. If the organization had a federal tax liability, the credit would offset the liability. If the organization did not have a federal tax liability, or its credits were in excess of its federal tax liability, it could apply for a refund of the liability.

Summary Conclusions

Children are sometimes without any health insurance protection. But the Coming of the Boomers will unravel the bizarre system of health insurance mostly based upon the workplace—which means even more children in coming decades face the prospect of losing health care insurance because their parents no longer receive health care insurance at their place of employment.

In the shorter term, the debate over welfare reform offers both dangers and opportunities. The danger is that more children could become uninsured or minimally insured as welfare recipients transfer to the workforce. A well-crafted plan to convert current Medicaid resources into a broader system of low-earner health insurance subsidies would not only overcome this danger but also extend health subsidies into a population with a high incidence of uninsurance.

Medical Savings Accounts are particularly well-suited for such a program. Former welfare recipients will learn responsible behavior quickly.

Also in the shorter term, the Earned Income Tax Credit as presently constructed is not a suitable vehicle for purchasing health insurance by low-earning families, primarily because of family liquidity constraints. Relatively simple modifications to the EITC, including the option of making it a transferable credit, would remove this barrier.

In the shortest of all terms, health insurance could be expanded by inducing state unemployment compensation departments routinely to inform the newly unemployed of their COBRA rights. Not all small businesses do this when an employee becomes unemployed, nor do many UC departments. Consequently, there are uninsured unemployed simply because they do not know of COBRA. This would be a simple, cheap, immediate step.

From a long-term view, we believe that the recently passed federal Kidcare (S-CHIP) legislation may complicate states' efforts to experiment with many of our short-term suggestions. Even though S-CHIP legislative architects insisted on including language that gives states flexibility in addressing the problem of uninsured kids, many states are simply using S-CHIP money to expand their current Medicaid programs. But S-CHIP does *not* mandate the creation of another insurance program, nor does it say that states must expand their Medicaid rolls with S-CHIP money.

We are concerned that as the employer-provided health care system begins its certain collapse early in the next century, parents and policymakers will look first to an institutionalized, state-level Kidcare solution to the problem of uninsured kids. And just as earlier Medicaid and Medicare cost projections were wildly under budget, Kidcare costs will begin to skyrocket in order to meet public demand. Parents, no longer receiving generous health care benefits at work, will understandably look wherever they can to find health care coverage for their children. Kidcare, with its promise of government-provided care for the children of parents too rich for Medicaid, will begin at first a gradual and then a rapid increase in growth, expanding into the middle class.

We argue in this chapter that as a society we must find suitable solutions to providing health care services to America's kids, who, through no fault of their own, lack adequate health care services. But when aging and retiring Boomers wreck the employer-provided health care market, more parents—including many middle-class parents—will lose their health care insurance. Which means the children of these parents will lose their health care coverage as well.

One of the biggest hurdles policymakers will face in coming years will be making health care services *easier* for parents and children to access by improving parents' *knowledge* of available health care services. Medicaid officials admit that their outreach to uninsured children eligible for Medicaid services but not enrolled in the program has been very poor. Other studies show that the main reasons children miss out on necessary health care services like immunizations are a lack of convenience and a lack of knowledge of health care programs on the part of children's parents.

Why not use some of the Kidcare dollars that will be flowing into state capital coffers over the next ten years to fund innovative programs targeting the twin problems of uninformed parents and inconvenient service delivery programs? Rather than simply expand Medicaid third-party insurance programs, states could create programs that get health care services directly into the neighborhoods of poor parents and their kids. Inner cities, which often must shoulder a higher burden in caring for poor children needing health care services, might use Kidcare funds to open community health centers. Or they might find value in funding a roving "Kids' Health" bus that could travel into impoverished neighborhoods knocking on doors, informing parents of existing child health care programs and perhaps offering free and immediate immunizations for children who have slipped through the health care cracks.

Our driving philosophy—detailed in this chapter and underlying our approach throughout this book—is to let innovation flourish. Policymakers have multiple choices for addressing children's health care needs. From refundable tax credits to MSAs for former welfare recipients, federal, state, and local policymakers should be open to considering a host of policy options for addressing the future health care needs of America's children.

But as always, the Boomers will drive the debate.

CHAPTER 4
THE CHALLENGE: AFFORDABLE ELDER CARE OPTIONS

Boomers will redo the sociodemographic landscape by virtue of their numbers (Chapter 1). Boomers will force the current health insurance system to
collapse (Chapter 2). Boomers will put great pressure on health care resources
available to children (Chapter 3). If Boomers hog available health care resources by demanding—and getting—every procedure and therapy for every
conceivable sickness, then the other part of the dependent population, children, may wind up shortchanged. There will be only so many health care resources to go around.

We would prefer this not be the case, but simple calculations suggest
otherwise.

Why the "Optimistic" Case Is Wrong

It was argued in the 1960s that a "rich" society such as the U.S. could
afford anything. Sometimes this is still asserted today. If we could put a man
on the moon, then we could afford anything. We could eradicate poverty, stop
pollution, assure everyone a good education, rescue decaying cities—fill in
your own blanks—and still leave families sufficient economic resources to
make familial decisions. John Kenneth Galbraith implied as much in his 1957
book, *The Affluent Society.*

Such assertions were false then and are false now. We have not eradicated
poverty. Our primary and secondary education system is worse. And we have
certainly not made the Great Society and New Deal promises for Medicare
and Social Security secure for the Baby Boomers, despite having spent tril-
lions of dollars more on these worthy causes.

Every first-year economics student is taught that we cannot have all the things we would like to have. The majority of us wouldn't mind owning Rolls Royces, living in mansions, eating lobster and caviar, spending the afternoons on sumptuous golf courses after spending the morning in an interesting job— and at the same time receiving the latest medical treatments from the greatest doctors in the world for whatever maladies afflict us.

Alas, this cannot happen. Scarcities, and how to allocate them, are a fact of life. There is no New Jerusalem on Earth. Some still suggest that economic growth might allow us to have all the health care we will want, for Boomers, children, and everyone else. A bit of reflection should call these assertions into question.

Given the recent historical per capita growth rates of the U.S. economy (about 2 percent, adjusted for inflation), by the year 2020 our national output of goods and services (GDP) will be about 52 percent higher than today. Why should it not be a simple matter to allocate a larger share of this much larger economic "pie" to take care of the Boomers, leaving younger workers with ample resources to take care of their own families—perhaps with a smaller share of the economic pie, but still more pie than they have in 1999?

We wish this were possible, but the argument falls apart upon examination.

The simple reason is that economic growth is *already* taken into account in official projections of payroll tax rates (of perhaps 37 percent by 2020 and over 50 percent by 2030) necessary to sustain the current Medicare and Social Security programs. One cannot count that same item twice. A child cannot spend a dollar on ice cream and expect it to be available for a candy bar.

Another "optimistic" argument concerns the "dependency ratio." This argument holds that what counts is not the ratio of the old to working-age populations, but rather the ratio of the total "dependent" population (children, adolescents, and the old) to the working-age population. Since the proportion of the 25-64 working-age population is expected to decline only modestly, from 51.6 percent in 1995 to 47.1 percent in 2020, the ratio of this population to "all others" does not change much. The proportion of those over 65 does rise dramatically, but this is largely offset by a reduction in the proportion of those under 25. Hence, there is little cause for alarm.

This argument is superficially appealing, but it too does not stand scrutiny. The cost of supporting a child (food, clothing, schoolbooks, toys, etc.) is a tiny fraction of the present cost of supporting an oldster, counting just Social Security alone. This is easiest to see in health care. After the first year of life, children are apt to require frequent physician care, but for things that are mostly easy and cheap to treat: childhood diseases which will "run their course"— earaches, sore throats, head lice, etc.—with only modest medical intervention.

Oldsters' complaints tend to be more chronic and require much more extensive and expensive interventions.

Although we sometimes lump the young and the old together in Chapter 3, in terms of the cost of maintaining them, they are *not* at all equivalent. The "dependent ratio" is no answer to the Boomer health care problem. We must look elsewhere.

The Imperative for Better Solutions

We reassert again that it is no exaggeration that one of America's great social policy challenges for the first half of the twenty-first century will be the attempted retirement of the 76 million Baby Boom generation. Indeed, it will be the *single* most important social policy challenge facing the country over the next three decades. The U.S. has never witnessed such an age-driven demographic tidal wave. As we struggle not to divide along race and gender lines, the possibility exists of intergenerational warfare if we do not carefully innovate new ways to take care of the elderly.

There are simply too many Boomers. We repeat again the inexorable demographic numbers. They are central to our understanding. The cohort born in 1945, the last year of World War II, numbers 2.8 million. That of 1946 is close to 3.8 million. After that, the Boomer cohorts hover at, above, or slightly below, 4 million. The first Boomers reach age 65 (what is now thought of as the "normal" retirement age) in the year 2011.

And there are too few Baby Busters to support them. Born in the two decades after 1964, these "Buster" cohorts gradually drop back to the 3-million-per-year level. They are the citizens who must support the Boomers. Current pensions and health care must be paid for from current production. There is no warehouse filled with the latest health care technology and the other good things of life labeled "for the consumption of the Baby Boom generation when they retire." The smaller size of the Buster generation shows up in many ways. As discussed in Chapter 1, Busters are the cause of the dramatic decline in elementary and secondary school enrollment beginning around 1972 and extending nearly to 1990. The relative imbalance in numbers between the Boomers and the Busters has already caused various social debates: for example, the problem of how much we should shrink the K-12 education infrastructure built to accommodate the Boomer generation.

Though many are at least vaguely aware of these age imbalances, the future implications for seniors, their public entitlements in general and health care entitlements in particular, are on the national radar screen. In its 1997 budget plan, the U.S. Senate took the daring step of proposing serious means testing for Medicare and a gradual increase in the full benefits retirement age from 65 to 67. Even though at one time the President indicated that he might be willing to go along with at least some of these proposals, nothing happened in the final package except to impose price controls on providers by further squeezing reimbursements.

Anyone who has examined the numbers realizes "cutting" Medicare and Social Security benefits is inevitable, either overtly by reducing benefits, or by raising full benefit retirement ages.

The demographics are stark. The previously referred to "Kerry Commission," chaired by Senators Robert Kerry (a Democrat) and John Danforth (a Republican) in 1994, brought this to light. But we should have known this anyway. Consider just the ratio of those in their prime working years, ages 25-64, to those over 65—i.e., the pool of potential workers to potential retirees. That ratio has been constant at roughly 4:1 for some decades and will stay there until 2010. When the first Boomers attempt to retire around 2011 (at age 65), it plummets to about 3:1 by the year 2020, and further erodes to close to 2:1 by the year 2030. It will stay at close to 2:1 for some decades after that.

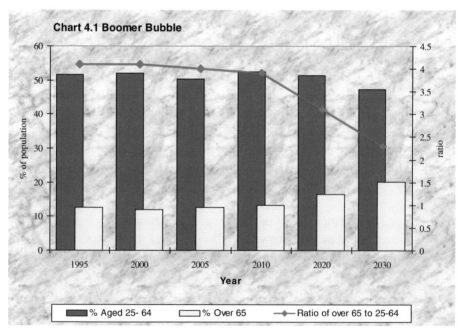

Source: Census Bureau projections. This chart has been presented earlier (Chapter 2), but is so crucial we restate it.

The ratio of *potential workers to potential retirees* will be cut in half in only the two decades from 2010 to 2030 (see Chart 4.1). We demonstrate this in Chapter 1. And we cannot ignore this demographic fact.

There is not much that social policy can do about this demographic trend.

Potential workers who will be alive in the year 2020 are already alive today. Barring massive changes in fertility rates, those who will be 25 and older in the year 2030 are also already mostly born. Changes in immigration policy might make marginal changes in the supply of productive employees, but only marginal.

Public policy regarding Medicare, Medicaid and Social Security thus assumes an urgent importance. Entitlements for seniors are destined to be cut back, no matter how many promises are made that they will be "protected." Under the Social Security Administration's "high-cost" projection, the payroll tax rate to maintain Medicare and Social Security at their current levels of generosity would have to increase to 37 percent in 2020 and to over 50 percent in 2030. Medicare—and health care for the elderly in general—is the more urgent priority of the two. In the absence of any legislative action to cut benefits, Medicare is scheduled to go "bankrupt" soon after the year 2008.

While Medicare costs are now lower per capita among the elderly, they are rising much faster than per capita Social Security costs.

Even this "high-cost" projection assumes that four of the five key variables necessary to project the future financial status of Medicare and Social Security (wages, medical prices, CPI inflation, longevity, and GDP growth) behave more favorably than they have over the last thirty years. While anything is possible, one does not make future personal financial plans on the assumption of winning the Powerball lottery.

And attempting to maintain current levels of senior entitlements also imply future confiscatory levels of taxation. Anything approaching, or exceeding, a 50 percent payroll tax rate by 2030 to maintain Social Security and Medicare at their current generosity levels is simply unthinkable. On top of this would be federal income taxes, and state and local property, sales, and income taxes. Taxation at these levels would be most unwise (and probably politically impossible in any case). The French have attempted to impose taxation at these marginal rates to maintain their welfare state. The result has been years of almost no economic growth, unemployment hovering between 11 percent and 13 percent, and not uncoincidentally rioting in the streets. The Socialist Party ironically has been voted back in to power.

Such ruinous taxation simply kills off all incentives to work, save, and invest.

The cost to the Baby Busters of trying to maintain the Boomers in their currently promised entitlements lifestyle will be crushing. The Busters' choices will be to emigrate, turn over an unacceptable share of their incomes to their parents, or hope for a decline in their parents' life spans. Boomers should find none of those choices appealing.

Why the Topic of this Chapter Is Important

Any member of the Baby Boom generation who has staked the core of his/her retirement plans on the current level of generosity of the elderly entitlement programs is doomed to disappointment.

In particular, the increasingly large population of the elderly that we will see over the next three decades demands some examination of whether there are medical care arrangements for the elderly that will be both more cost-effective and "good" for the client. Medicare and the parts of Medicaid dealing with the elderly, particularly nursing homes, will come under increasing pressure. Washington D.C. is beginning to bestir itself with talk of the inevitable "cuts" in benefits (disguised under the term "reform"). If there are no such "better answers," the demographic implosion will force serious changes in the U.S. health care system. And not to the advantage of the numerous and increasingly angry Baby Boom generation, which will be watching its Social Security and Medicare promises melt away. Are there better ways to care for the elderly?

For some years, Indiana has had in place a relatively comprehensive home health care plan, the "In-Home/CHOICE" program. CHOICE is an acronym for Community and Home Health Care Options for the Elderly and Disabled. Presumably this not quite accurate acronym was picked because it resonated.

CHOICE is a Home Health Care (HHC) program entirely funded by the state as a last resort if all other federally funded HHC options, whether the funding is total or partial, fail to fit the needs of the elderly client or if his or her financial resources are exhausted.

The theory behind the HHC concept is that with a bit of help—with medical equipment, assistance in the activities of daily living, or meals—an elderly person might be able to remain in his or her home and avoid costly institutionalization. Theoretically, everyone wins. By paying for relatively modest costs of HHC, taxpayers avoid paying for full nursing home institutionalization. The elderly person remains in the old homeplace, where many would prefer to be.

The question is whether the theory is borne out by the facts.

We conducted an in-depth study of the Indiana In-Home/CHOICE program. This plan is known nationally as among the best HHC schemes. It has received research support from the Robert Wood Johnson Foundation and has been a popular program with the Indiana state legislature. But does it really work? The expansion of the program by a generally conservative state legislature (see below) is not, in and of itself, evidence that the program "works." After all, most people would like something free from the government (i.e., from the rest of us). The elderly are no exception. But as a society groping for ways to deal with the future waves of the Boomer generation, we must be prepared to experiment with alternative health care delivery systems.

The authors are no great philosophical fans of more government involvement in the health care system. But we did not write this book to satisfy our biases. Medicaid and Medicare are there. They will not be repealed soon, if ever. As long as they are there, we should search for economist Mancur Olson's "theory of the second best." How do we best deliver health care to the aging Boomers so as to maximize health care delivery to the young and their children?

The authors were initially quite skeptical of claims that the In-Home/ CHOICE plan is really that "win-win" situation where both the elderly and the taxpayers are better off. After examining the evidence, we find strong indications that the In-Home/CHOICE program is an example of how an HHC program can fulfill its theoretical promise. Many other HHC programs have quite legitimately come under fire for ballooning costs, fraud, and abusive overuse. What we find in this study is strong presumptive evidence—not conclusive evidence, but highly indicative—that at least some of the claims for HHC as *potentially* both "better" and "cheaper" than full institutionalization have a basis in fact. HHC, if properly crafted and administered, has a potentially vital role to play in helping our society cope with the looming health care needs of the Baby Boomers. This is a topic that deserves national discussion beyond recent negative reports of other HHC programs which have perhaps not been as well-designed.

Home Health Care in Particular

Let's begin with the example of "Susie Smith." "Susie" (not her real name) is a real person. She is 82 years old and has trouble bathing herself. She has trouble combing her hair. If someone helps with the grocery shopping, she can get a meal into the microwave. She says (no one knows for sure, short of sending in the mythical Elderly Police) that she has no friends or relatives to help her out. She could well be in a nursing home.

In an Intermediate Care nursing home facility, "Susie" would cost about $27,000 to the taxpayers, based upon the 1996 average for Indiana facilities. "Susie" gets about $7,000 from the In-Home/CHOICE program in services to maintain her in her residence. Someone comes (most of the time) to help her with the things she can no longer do for herself. When asked in a Quality Assurance program survey, "Susie" says she is happy with the program.

"Susie" is how an HHC program is theoretically supposed to work. "Susie" is happy to remain in her own home. The costs of institutionalization would be $20,000 higher.

"Susie" also illustrates the limits of our knowledge. We observe that "Susie" gets help from the CHOICE program and remains in her own home. But this could be a *post hoc ergo propter hoc* (i.e., after it therefore because of it) fallacy. Maybe Susie fudged a little in telling an interviewer about her infirmities. Maybe she does have a relative who could help out, and public money is merely supplanting what would otherwise be a familial (and socially healthy) obligation. Maybe she so loathes the idea of institutionalization that she would stick it out at home almost no matter what. We can never be *absolutely* certain that publicly funded HHC is the critical variable in keeping "Susie" out of a nursing home.

Still, we can observe that "Susie" is at home. We also observe that a lot of "Susies" do eventually need institutional care—at a much higher cost to the taxpayer—when relatively modest HHC interventions no longer suffice. With a cost-differential ratio of 27:7 between institutionalization and HHC, nearly three out of four "Susies" would have to be fudging about the extent of their infirmities or family status for the program not to make financial sense. No doubt some of that happens. There is abuse in any public program. But it is unlikely to be that rampant. And "Susie" reveals a preference for avoiding an institution by the simple act of remaining in her own home. What we demonstrate in this chapter is a high *probability* that the Indiana In-Home/CHOICE program is a model that policymakers should seriously consider copying as one of the tools to make the retirement years of the Baby Boomers tolerable.

Home Health Care in General

Home health care has been an extensively debated topic. Over 1600 popular and academic articles have appeared in the last eighteen months alone (as determined by the Hudson Institute Research Library). Doubtless there are others our research has not uncovered.

HHC is intended to be the first step in a chain of interventions designed to avoid institutionalization. HHC in theory is followed up the non-institutionalization chain by assisted-living arrangements, group homes, hospices, and rehabilitation. In practice, however, there are few programs available between home health care and an institution.

Public money spent on HHC has been expanding at nearly 20 percent per year. Medicare spending alone grew from $1.9 billion in 1988 to $9.7 billion in 1994. Such explosive growth in outlays has inevitably attracted the notice of congressional budget cutters and General Accounting Office auditors.

Numbers of clients of HHC nationally are growing by leaps and bounds. There were 1.5 million HHC clients in 1993, up from 1.2 million in 1992. Three-quarters were over age 65 and two-thirds were female. Every year since then, Indiana and the Indiana General Assembly, the units of study for the In-Home/CHOICE program in this chapter, has increased the number of CHOICE recipients by an average of 10 percent per year. Clearly, there is something of note happening here.

The Indiana Program

Indiana began experiments in 1985 with a trial HHC program in fifteen of Indiana's ninety-two counties. The program proved extremely popular with the public and the state legislature. By State Fiscal Year 1993 (1 July 1992-30 June 1993), the program had been expanded by the legislature to all ninety-two counties. It began with a demonstration/trial project grant of less than $1 million and has expanded to over $20 million in ten years.

Table 4.2
Hierarchy of Preferred Programs and "Slots": FY 1995.

Program	Number of Participants
Social Services Bloc Grants	73,145
Title III, Older Americans Act	23,295
Medicaid Waivers	2,725
CHOICE	5,208

This a remarkable expansion for *any* public program in a state that has a (deserved) reputation for being among the most fiscally conservative in the nation. Indiana's current state budget surplus exceeds $2.7 billion, the largest per capita of any state by a wide margin. As a rule, public-spending programs do not grow very much in Indiana unless they are unavoidable federal mandates. Thus, even if In-Home/CHOICE were nothing else, it would be an interesting political case study.

Mechanically, the program is quite simple. A state level agency, the Family and Social Services Administration, oversees the program from an office in Indianapolis. This agency provides general supervision and contracts with sixteen Area Agencies on Aging ("AAAs"). The AAAs are not-for-profit and vary somewhat in their own governance. Two are state universities. AAAs in turn purchase HHC from various providers for their clients in that area.

At any one time, AAAs employ a total of approximately 400 case managers. Case managers interview prospective clients via a standardized questionnaire. The questionnaire is a key quality control point. It is designed to minimize the number of "Susies" who overtly fudge about their condition. The case managers then determine whether the applicant meets eligibility criteria, and the services which are appropriate are determined.

Table 4.3
Outlays by Category: State Fiscal Year 1996

Program	Amount
Medicaid Waiver	$28,444,597
CHOICE	$20,676,425
Soc. Services Bloc Grant	$10,078,364
Title III, Older Americans	$8,834,382

Source: Indiana State Budget Agency documents.

But there is a question of whether resources to pay for these services are adequate for everyone who "wants in" and out of what "pot" of money their services will be paid. Budget officials at any level of government are always seeking to use the maximum amounts of someone else's money—in this case, federal. (Federal budget officials, of course, naturally always wish states and localities to pay. This is a game that can traced back as far as the Emperor Diocletian.) Once an AAA case worker determines an interviewee is eligible for In Home/CHOICE help, he or she will run through a hierarchy of the four main "pots" of money available for the overall program, beginning with the category which contains the "most" federal money and ending with the CHOICE program, which is 100 percent state-funded. CHOICE, as purely a state program, will not be used then unless none of the other three fully or partially federal programs is either tapped out or will not pay for the needed service.

Expenditures do not parallel numbers of recipients for a particular program because of different intensity levels of services provided. For example, to qualify for a Medicaid waiver (established in the late 1980s by the Omnibus Budget Reconciliation Act) there must be an explicit calculation that the cost of institutionalization is greater than the cost of HHC services. These are persons who are normally sicker and/or more infirm with a correspondingly higher per capita cost. It should be noted that there are other waivers, such as for autism or Intermediate Care for the Mentally Retarded (ICF/MR), but the aging waiver is by far the most prevalent.

Table 4.4
Final Disposition of a Sample of CHOICE Cases.

Reason	Number	Percent
Death	1,026	29.2
Institutionalization	992	28.2
Other (unspecified)	942	26.8
Went on Medicaid Waiver	177	5.0
Improved Health	162	4.8
Moved	155	4.4
Refused Cost Share	63	1.8
Total	3,517	100.0

Source: Data are taken from 8 of the 16 Indiana AAA's from all available documentation.

CHOICE, the state program, is a bit more liberal in its program admission standards than nursing home admission requirements for Medicaid funded nursing home admission. There are six recognized and required deficits in Activities of Daily Living (ADL). They are:
• Requires assistance in bathing;
• Requires assistance in dressing;
• Requires assistance in using toilet;
• Requires assistance in transferring;
• Has difficulty with bowel/bladder control;
• Requires assistance in eating.
Medicaid requires a minimum of three of the above six ADL impairments for nursing home eligibility. The National Nursing Home Survey shows that nursing home residents average 3.8 ADL restrictions and three out of five residents have four or more. In July 1995 (Public Law 150), the eligibility criteria for the CHOICE program was reduced from three to two ADL restrictions. Thus, a CHOICE recipient technically could receive services even if not qualified for a nursing home.

However, when a sample is taken of the final disposition of CHOICE recipients, a quite interesting pattern emerges.

Table 4.4 is highly suggestive. The largest group leaves the program via death. But the average stay in the CHOICE program is not long; over half are in the program less than a year. If death follows so quickly, this group on balance is more than likely quite sick or debilitated when entering the program. The large majority would no doubt qualify for nursing home admittance in the absence of CHOICE. As with our example of "Susie," this is not possible to prove without a multi-year longitudinal study. However, Occam's Razor, the logical principle that the simplest explanation is usually the best, makes this by far the most likely explanation.

The second largest group of "leavers" eventually does wind up in an institution. Here the evidence is even more suggestive. CHOICE apparently buys some period of time of cheaper, home-bound care before further health deterioration makes institutionalization unavoidable.

The third largest group comprises those whose available records are not sufficient to determine the reason for leaving. The remainder fall into one or another miscellaneous category, such as moving. Thus, there is strong evidence that, even though a CHOICE recipient might not qualify for nursing home admittance, many—almost certainly a large majority—would in fact do so.

Costs

The theory behind the CHOICE program is that home health is usually cheaper than institutionalization in that it *saves money for the state*, even though the program is entirely state-funded, whereas institutionalization would be matched by federal dollars at a rate that accounts for about two-thirds of the total cost. (Thus, the federal treasury gets a free ride for every recipient who is in CHOICE and not a Medicaid waiver.)

Table 4.5
Average Cost Per Recipient, CHOICE Versus Nursing Home (Indiana State Fiscal Year 1996).

	Average CHOICE Cost		Average Medicaid Nursing Home Reimbursement		
			Weighted	Skilled	Intermediate
Annual Cost	Elderly	Disabled	Total	Nursing	Nursing
State Share	$6623	$8318	$6994	$13,616	$10,075
Federal Share	0	0	0	$22,762	$16,842

These differences are not minor. Consider the absolute "worst case" scenario, a disabled person who might otherwise need only an intermediate care nursing home. The ratio of costs is still better than 10:8 *for state funds only* as between institutionalization and the CHOICE home care alternative. When federal funds are counted, the ratio is 27:8. For an elderly person, on average the ratio is 14:7 considering only state funds, and 36:7 counting federal funds. While we analyze at length earlier in this study why we cannot be certain that every CHOICE recipient would otherwise be institutionalized, we have presented evidence that large numbers of them otherwise would be. Given the large cost-differentials between the CHOICE program and even the lower end of institutionalization, it is almost inconceivable that the program is not cost-effective.

Quality Assurance

There is considerable discussion about abuses of the Medicare component of HHC. The General Accounting Office has released a report criticizing the Health Care Financing Administration and many state HHC administrations for admitting "almost anyone" as a HHC provider. The report charges that claimed and billed visits are sometimes not made, and that when they are made the quality of service is sometimes substandard. Recipients are seldom queried about the service provided. (See *inter alia, The New York Times*, 27 July 1997).

While the GAO report is certainly correct in observing that getting "customer" feedback is an elementary technique of good management, the criticism does not apply to the In-Home/CHOICE program. In 1995, The Robert Wood Johnson Foundation (TRWJF) funded a client feedback program for the In-Home/CHOICE program, the Quality Improvement Program for Home-Based Care. The theory is simple. First establish a rigorous questionnaire to make certain that most persons who enter the program actually belong there. Then ask the recipients whether they are actually receiving the services they need in a timely manner.

A sample of recipients has been and is being asked to rate the timeliness and quality of care they receive. Sanctions, including decertification from the program, are taken against those providers who consistently fare poorly on the survey. TRWJF anticipated the GAO's criticisms by two years. Customer feedback, as opposed to central office paper-shuffling, is a necessary item for an HHC program to work. The GAO report simply points out that such actions are infrequently taken.

Table 4.6 points out that such actions *have* already been taken in the In-Home/CHOICE program. In Table 4.6, a score of 1 is "never;" a score of 2 is "occasionally;" a score of 3 is "half of the time;" a score of 4 is "usually;" a score of 5 is "always."

Several points are worthy of note. The number of respondents differs for several reasons. First, not all respondents receive a particular service (e.g., meals, transportation). Second, these data are taken from the initial (and at that point, experimental) client response project, and several different survey techniques were used, with different questions.

All of the scores are high. The score for respect and trustworthiness of the care provided is outstanding. When someone the recipient trusts shows up, all goes well. The two relatively low scores (below 4, but still very good) are shown first, for consistency. That is not surprising. There is a high personnel turnover for some types of services in the HHC business

The second "low score" is for the quality of meals—close to "usually good." Any number of interpretations can be put on this datum. One would be that meals prepared by someone else, other than Mom's home cooking, are never quite up to par for anyone, from Roman legionnaire soldiers to modern-day college students.

Table 4.6
Client Outcome Measures
Client Satisfaction with Services
CHOICE and Medicaid Aged and Waiver Clients*(1996)

Component: Satisfaction with Attendant Care, Home Health Aides, and/or Homemaker Services	Number of Respondents	Outcomes Score
Degree of choice/autonomy	3809	4.75
Consistency/ Services and Workers	1906	3.95
Respectfulness/ Trustworthiness of Workers	6222	4.91
Timeliness	2866	4.55
Quality of Task Performance	4327	4.68
Quality of Home Delivered Meals	905	3.89
Quality of Transportation Service	178	4.88

Note: This is not original research. These data are taken from the original project funded by The Robert Wood Johnson Foundation.

It is quite easy to survey recipients about their satisfaction levels with HHC. One just needs to do it. It has been done in Indiana with the CHOICE program, and can be done elsewhere. If recipients are as satisfied as they seem to be, then that is a more important consideration than the satisfaction of any bureaucracy with i-dotting and t-crossing regulations.

What Next?

We have presented here evidence that a well-conceived, publicly-funded HHC program can be a superior alternative to publicly-funded institutionalization for the coming wave of Baby Boomer retirees. Indiana's In-Home/CHOICE program is an example. One must properly screen applicants to ensure that they are truly eligible and follow up with customer surveys as the best means of quality control.

Just how much money can be "saved" by such plans as opposed to institutionalization?

That answer is necessarily speculative. Indiana is a rather typical state in many respects (it has about 2 percent of national population, 2 percent of personal income, for example) and is thus a good barometer for extrapolating to national numbers.

But we must also return to "Susie Smith." We still don't know for certain that every "Susie" would wind up in an institution. Some assumptions have to be made. Suppose half of all "Susies" would not be institutionalized even without In-Home/CHOICE intervention. That means that for every $7,000 average investment in a "Susie" that keeps her out of an institution, another $7,000 is spent on a "Susie" who would have stayed at home anyway. That is still only $14,000 spent to avoid the average $27,000 cost of low-level institutionalization, a savings of not quite 50 percent. This is significant money.

Public home health care outlays are fated to expand. The concept appears to be facing teething troubles from rapid expansion. It is a good concept. It can also, and has been, abused. The "critical control points" are the intake questionnaire and the feedback of recipients. Critical control points mimic the modern conception of inspecting to assure safe food. Forget about relatively trivial concerns, such as grease spots on the restaurant's wall, and concentrate on those things that count, such as making certain the turkey is being cooked to a proper temperature.

HHC can save at least $5 billion per year nationally for Medicare even under 1996 outlays and a good—but not perfect—HHC system such as the Indiana In-Home/CHOICE plan.

One should also recognize that there is, of course, a moral hazard in any public program. Everyone would "like to have" all the good things in life at someone else's expense. HHC's eligibility criteria must remain at levels where HHC intervention is likely to make the difference between home living and institutionalization.

Home Health Care can be a powerful weapon in helping the nation afford the retirement years of the Baby Boom generation.

Our purpose in writing this chapter has been to show that there *are* alternatives to the current health care delivery system for the Boomers that are both embraced by the elderly and cheaper for the taxpayers. It is not perfect, but it is better. If we hope to survive the onslaught of the Boomer retirees, we must find more.

CHAPTER 5
BIOETHICS

Bioethics: the study of moral issues in medical research and treatment.

—Webster's Dictionary

As with all other issues regarding America's health care system in the early twenty-first century, aging Boomers will stoke the fires of the bioethics debate. Bioethics, the study of moral issues in the fields of medical treatment and research, will be increasingly important in coming decades. How much expensive cutting-edge medical care will all of those aged Boomers receive?

Karen Ann Quinlan was a drug interaction victim who had been pronounced clinically brain dead. Nearly twenty years ago television's evening news shows reported for months on the saga of whether she should be allowed to die. A new marvelous medical machine, the respirator, was keeping her alive. Her parents wanted her disconnected from the machine. Her doctors argued that their medical ethics required them to prolong life to the best of their ability. Eventually the case was resolved in court. The parents won and the "plug was pulled." The extensive media coverage over whether Karen Ann Quinlan's life should be prolonged indefinitely with no hope of recovery made many Americans think about "bioethics," even if they had never heard of the word.

In this chapter we discuss bioethics and provide a brief historical review of how we have dealt with bioethical dilemmas in the past. We discuss how rapid biotechnological advances might impact the health care options of all Americans, paying particular attention to the bioethical dilemmas created by the aging of the Baby Boomers.

As we creep closer to the twenty-first century America's health care environment is in an era of astonishing change. The confluence of biological research, rapid technological advances, and the aging of the Baby Boomers will intensify the bioethical debate in our society. However, we caution the reader that there are no easy answers to this bioethical policy pickle. There are no solutions to the bioethical dilemmas of coming years that will satisfy everyone. But we cannot hide from the bioethical debate. It is here today and will only be more explosive by 2020.

The Bioethics Debate

Bioethics deals with ethical and moral issues in the life sciences and the controversies involved in distributing scarce medical resources in a society. While the complexity of the bioethics debate has accelerated dramatically in recent years, the underlying issues involved are not new.

The ancient Greek Hippocratic Oath, for example, was an early code of ethics, counseling physicians above all to "do no harm" in caring for patients. Following World War II, the Nuremburg Code for medical research ethics sprang out of the horrors of human experimentation carried out by Nazi death-camp doctors. Outrage at the federal government's secret Tuskegee Study (which withheld effective treatment options for black men during a forty-year study of the clinical course of syphilis) further pushed the public's concern with bioethical issues onto the national agenda.

Today, it seems a news cycle hardly passes without reports of a revolutionary advance in biomedical research that brings up thorny bioethical questions. We were stunned, for example, to hear the first "Baaahhh" from "Dolly" the cloned sheep in the late 1990s. But Dolly is not alone.

Researchers in Virginia recently welcomed into the world "Rosie," a transgenic calf whose milk contains a human protein that might help premature infants who have trouble nursing. Wisconsin scientists have genetically altered turkey hens to increase their egg productivity. Researchers in Florida have created and released a genetically engineered predator mite that is expected to gobble up other mites that are destroying strawberry crops.

Biotechnological discoveries are advancing at dizzying rates. "Dolly," "Rosie," and their genetically manipulated cousins each represent dramatic biotechnological advances that have direct consequences for humans, their health care, and the bioethic debate in coming decades.

Some have argued that as a result of biotechnological advances our very way of life will be more fundamentally transformed in coming decades than it has in the previous one thousand years. (See, for example, Jeremy Rifkin, *The Biotech Century* (1998); Joseph Coates et al., *2025* (1997); and "Fabricating Human Organs is No Longer Science Fiction,"

Sunday Times [London], 23 November 1997*).* When scientists fully unravel and code the entire genome of the approximately 100,000 human
genes early in the next century an explosion of human biotechnological
applications may be possible. Some futurists predict that human genome
research will reveal the linkages between all human diseases and disorders
by 2020. Others suggest that customized genetic changes to cell DNA,
either before conception, just after conception in the embryonic cells, or
during fetal development might be not only clinically possible but conceivably commonplace by early in the next century. And others predict
that by the year 2020, 95 percent of human body parts—including lungs,
hearts, livers, and pancreases—will be candidates for replacement by labo-
ratory-grown organs of human cells.

Confidently forecasting the pace of biotechnological changes is beyond the scope of the authors' expertise and of our interest in writing this
book. However, the underlying bioethical issues and health policy questions resulting from a likely acceleration in biotechnological developments
in the future cannot be avoided.

If the past is prologue, then perhaps it is useful to look at how Americans
have previously dealt with perplexing bioethical issues. Thus we next consider two medical device advances—iron lungs and dialysis machines—and
discuss how Americans dealt with the bioethical issues entangled in their introduction to society.

Bioethical Dilemmas in the Past: Iron Lungs and Kidney Dialysis Machines

Two historical examples give some instruction about how the U.S. has
dealt with past medical scarcity: "iron lungs" and kidney dialysis machines.

Prior to Dr. Jonas Salk's development of an effective vaccine in 1954,
the poliomyelitis virus was the dread of every parent. The virus attacked
the intercostal muscles of the diaphragm. Breathing was impeded, often
fatally. The disease was correctly perceived as a children's disease: almost
all victims were children or teenagers, and two-thirds were under age 9.

In 1928, Philip Drinker, a Harvard applied physiologist, perfected a
device that could take over a patient's breathing for long periods of time.
The patient was placed in a large metal tank (hence the term "iron lung")
with an airtight rubber collar around the neck. Alternate positive and negative air pressure caused the patient to "breathe." Although the iron lung
was effective for only one type of polio, intercostal paralytic polio, in which
the intercostal muscles of the diaphragm eventually regain their breathing
function, it quickly came to be regarded as the world's first medical "miracle

machine." Actual results for mortality and morbidity were poor, but a few highly publicized survival cases caused a clamor for iron lungs in every locale.

But iron lungs were expensive, and not every locale could afford them. A possibly lifesaving therapy was being denied and, moreover, being denied to vulnerable children.

Stepping into the void was the National Foundation for Infantile Paralysis (NFIP), better known as the March of Dimes. NFIP was founded in 1937 by Franklin Delano Roosevelt, himself a polio victim. Its initial goal was to fund research into polio (the NFIP would underwrite the research that produced the first polio vaccine) and to make sure clinical services were available to polio victims. In 1941, NFIP decided to add the goal of making an iron lung available to every patient who might conceivably benefit from its use.

NFIP was one of the most successful private charities ever. In its first eleven years of operation, it raised almost $600 million (when a dollar was worth almost six times as much as today). NFIP boasted 4,000 local chapters and over 100,000 volunteers. Iron lungs proliferated, so much that they became *over*used. When faced with a gasping patient with bulbar polio (where no recovery of breathing function would occur because of brain cell damage), some physicians opted to put the patient into an iron lung. This, of course, doomed the child to spend his remaining days—sometimes months or even years—in a metal prison with a quality of life essentially zero. Some patients eventually rebelled and asked to be allowed to die.

The essential point is that a private charity did overcome the scarcity. From the rationing of iron lungs, NFIP instead provided an overabundance. Private charity worked.

Kidney dialysis machines give us a second clue. Renal failure is rare among children. In this case, the onset of End State Renal Disease (ESRD) disease is seldom before middle age.

Use of machines to cleanse the blood of fatal impurities caused by nonfunctioning kidneys was perfected by 1938. The catch was that each intervention by the machine required a surgical procedure on veins and arteries to divert blood flow to the machine. After a short period of time, surgeons ran out of blood vessels with which they could work. These early kidney machines were good only for sustaining a patient over a few weeks until the kidneys began to function again. They were useless for patients with long-term, chronic kidney failure.

All of this changed in 1960. Dr. Belding Scribner of the University of Washington Medical School devised a way to give a patient a permanent "hook-up point" to a dialysis machine without blood vessel surgery. He used the marvelous new material Teflon, which many Americans have on their pots and pans. Teflon is so chemically inert that it can be safely implanted into the human body with no rejection effects (it also does not react with bacon grease or anything else cooked in a Teflon-coated pan, which is why Teflon is prized by cooks around the world).

No more repeated surgeries were to occur. Permanent treatment of terminally ill, and heretofore untreatable, chronic renal patients was at hand. Hook them up to a dialysis machine several times a week and outwardly they would seem to be as healthy as anyone else. ESRD patients now sensed a chance.

But as in the case of the iron lung, long-term renal dialysis was prohibitively expensive. Initially, each treatment required an eight-hour hospital stay on the machine, several times a week for the rest of the patient's life. The machine itself was expensive, and insurance companies were understandably loathe to write insurance to cover such an expense for the thirty or forty years of a patient's remaining normal life expectancy.

The NFIP's private charity solution was not possible. These patients were not young children to be helped by the March of Dimes. They were mostly older people who, it could be argued, had already lived a good part of their productive lives. Moreover, their numbers were much fewer than the number of prevaccine polio victims and parents. How did this group of renal dialysis victims respond?

They responded by turning their relatively small, but committed, numbers to their advantage. They appealed to the federal government for funding for dialysis machines. One dialysis patient calmly testified before a U.S. Senate Committee while hooked up to a portable dialysis machine. The result was Section 2991 of the Social Security Act of 1972, in which Congress agreed to pay for all costs of treating ESRD (still the only terminal disease for which the taxpayers are asked to give *carte blanche* for prolonged technology-intensive treatment).

Lessons?

Iron lungs and renal dialysis are two *specific* cases dealing with a *specific* shortage of medical technology. (Managed care is a more general case, which we discussed earlier.) Society dealt with the former through private charity, the latter through federal largess for a relatively small part of the population. Neither can be applied to the Boomer health care problem. The private charity model used to purchase iron lungs is not apt to work for a society-wide phenomenon such as the Boomers. Organized charity can buy iron lungs. It will not buy all the high-tech medical care all of the Boomers think they want and need.

Nor is the renal dialysis model of much help. An appeal to the federal budget may work for a small group of people with a highly visible disease. It cannot work, for reasons we gave in Chapter 2, for the Boomers. Their old age health care will be part of a larger old age health and retirement problem. An entire generation of historically large Baby Boomer numbers on expanded Medicare-as-we-know-it is not in the cards.

A key bioethical dilemma is that iron lungs treated children with their entire lives before them. No society has ever scrimped in protecting its children. At first, renal dialysis patients began as mostly adults in their productive middle age. By 2020, the first decade Boomers will be old, with a limited life span. Providing every conceivable treatment to them will literally result in a Health Care Economy, perhaps 25 percent of Gross Domestic Product by 2020 and 30 percent of GDP by 2030. If the Boomers pay from their own pockets or from their own insurance policies or Medical Savings Accounts, there is nothing *ipso facto* wrong with this. But what if the aged Boomers insist that the young pay for their health care through the public budget?

Since the historical examples of iron lungs and dialysis machines are of little help, we must look elsewhere for answers.

Bioethical Dilemma of the Future: Boomer Access to Advanced Medical Devices, an Example

Early in the next century America's Baby Boomers will wish to retire from America's workforce. When and if they do leave the workforce, they may not want to slow down. But their bodies will.

Does this mean that by the year 2020 millions of now-geezer Boomers will soon be lining up in doctors' offices for the most advanced medical devices and procedures to mend their aching joints? They may try to, but it is problematic whether all of them will get what they seek.

The American public is just now becoming aware of the implications of the rapidly aging, and soon-to-be retiring, Baby Boom generation. With an aging population there should be a boom in demand for advanced medical procedures in coming decades. But fundamental inconsistencies in the provision of health care services in our country threaten the ability of patients to make choices regarding their health care.

When needing advanced medical treatments, aging Baby Boomers may find that they are limited in their choice of doctor, surgical procedure, or surgical device. Managed care cost-cutting and additional government health care mandates could lead to the future rationing of health care services that would make today's HMO complaints seem mild, forcing patients to lose their right to choose the best treatment plans and doctors to lose their ability to counsel patients in this choice.

Demographic trends suggest a major increase in Boomer demand for advanced medical procedures in coming years. Many aging Boomers, for instance, will have ground down their joints. A surge in demand for knee and hip replacements is projected to occur soon after 2015.

One advanced medical procedure we would logically expect aging Boomers to demand is Total Joint Replacement (TJR). Total joint replacement is performed when an arthritic or damaged joint (most commonly at the hip or knee) is removed and replaced with an artificial joint or prosthesis. A smooth layer of cartilage covers the bone ends of a joint. Under normal functioning, the cartilage allows for frictionless and pain-free movement. But when the cartilage is damaged or diseased by arthritis, these joints can become rigid and painful. Total joint replacement can become necessary when other treatment options cannot relieve the pain and disability of the damage done to this cartilage.

In recent years TJR—in particular total hip and total knee replacement— has become an increasingly common surgical procedure. Between 1976 and 1995 there were well over 3 million total hip replacements and close to 3 million total knee replacements.

One would logically expect that aging Baby Boomer Americans will desire medical procedures such as TJR. But intensifying pressure on health care resources could lead to some of them being turned away.

The traditional doctor-patient relationship has been damaged in recent years. The gradual shift in focus in American health care away from a stress on the importance of quality care and toward an emphasis on cutting costs has serious implications for health care in America. Managed care is one form of rationing. It is in the private sector and thus becomes a convenient target for political attack. Managed care cost-cutting and government health care mandates are already forcing the rationing of many health care services, and will do so increasingly. Patients could increasingly lose their right to choose the best medical procedures. Doctors could increasingly lose their ability to counsel patients in this choice.

Patients, unaware of and thus unprepared for the imminent crisis in health care financing that retiring Baby Boomers will cause in the coming decades, may lose their ability to choose medical procedures that best serve their needs.

This means there might be millions of aching Boomers unable to access the best medical advice, products, and procedures to mend their painful hips and knees and other afflictions of old age.

The Boomers and Bioethics: No Good Answers

Since this book focuses primarily on the Baby Boomers and how the aging of America will forever change the way we finance and deliver health care services, it is useful to speculate on how the bioethical debate in America might proceed over the next few decades. When the Baby Boomers transform into retiring geezers early in the next century, how might the bioethical debate evolve? Ultimately, who gets to "play God" in making health care decisions for America's aging Boomers?

Thanks to improved medical diagnoses, medical treatments, and lifestyle choices, we are living longer. The normal retirement age of 65 was picked by Otto Von Bismarck, Chancellor of Prussia, in the late 1880s because few lived to that age. If they did, they were likely not to live much longer. And if current government projections are correct, Americans in the next few decades will be living even longer than they do today. The Kerry Commission (see Chapter 2) warned us of this near-certain expansion of the numbers of older Americans. Life expectancy for Americans in 1960 stood at just over 70 years. By the mid-1990s we were living on average nearly 76 years, and by 2025, even leaving aside the possible development of any unforeseen medical breakthroughs, it is estimated we will live on average over 78 years. Further, in 1965, when an American reached age 65 he or she could expect to live another 14.6 years. By 2025, those reaching age 65 will live on average another 18.8 years.

We introduced this chapter by defining the bioethics debate as dealing with ethical and moral issues in the life sciences and the controversies involved in distributing scarce medical resources in a society. We stress again, however, that there are no easy answers in these bioethics debates. No bioethicist has the solution that will satisfy everyone. When the Baby Boomers' bodies begin to degenerate early in the next century public policymakers will be confronted with a policy dilemma of enormous proportions.

As we discussed in Chapter 2, Medicare, barring massive changes in its fundamental design, will be unable to care for every need of every aging Boomer. We already divert tremendous financial resources to caring for the oldest Americans in their final years of life. (The National Committee for Quality Health Care reported that even back in the early 1990s nearly 30 percent of total Medicare expenditures were occurring during the final year of life.) Will every single Baby Boomer be able to afford every heroic effort biotechnological advances might make available to the doctors of 2020?

Current Thinking

The current bioethics discussion offers few clues. Indeed, it does not go much beyond ideas which the average American would advance if forced to think about it. And the average American would not like any of them. Here are some examples.

Daniel Callahan of the Hastings Center suggested that once a person reaches an appropriate old age that person should receive only palliative care, not the latest technology. When medical care threatens to swallow up resources necessary to keep the political and legal systems functioning, the line has been crossed. Callahan's argument has flaws, not the least of which is determining (at what age and by whom) the location of that mystical line where one crosses over and beyond an appropriate old age. Is the mere fact that Nobel Laureate economist Milton Friedman is approaching his tenth decade sufficient to disqualify him from access to the best possible treatments—even though he still contributes lucid articles to *The Wall Street Journal*?

John Kilner and Paul Menzel advocate a lottery system for rationing medical resources. Left unanswered is just who should be allowed into the lottery, and for whom there should be any lottery at all. Only those over age 50 who are dying? Only those over age 70 who might be in danger of death? Only those over age 60 whose quality of life might improve? The devil is in the details, and the details evoke as much rancor as the original question of who gets what services. Menzel also advocated a "duty to die cheaply." The obvious but also unanswered questions are "Whose duty?" and "How cheap?"

Others have attempted to "quantify" the problem. Dr. William Knaus of Harvard developed a computer program to "predict" patient outcomes based on age and prior medical history. Those with a low probability of some kind of favorable recovery would receive lowest priority in allocation of scarce treatments. A 90-year-old with diabetes and two past heart attacks who is admitted to a hospital with a diagnosis of a moderate stroke might be predicted to have only a 5 percent chance of a meaningful recovery. But what of the 5 percent chance? And what if that patient or relatives were willing to pay for the 5 percent chance? Must we all die equally because of data from a computer program?

There are many others who have written on bioethics, and our intent is not to disparage any of the persons we have mentioned. We only illustrate that we have yet to find any "good" answer to the bioethics dilemma that will begin to consume our society as the Boomers age.

What Does the Bioethics Future Look Like?

One safe prediction is that, if you are asked by your son or daughter for a growth industry he or she might enter, bioethics would be a good choice.

Another safe prediction is that bioethics must and will emerge from a narrow perspective of "how to allocate the scarcity" of medical services and into a broader questioning of health insurance, alternative health care delivery systems (e.g., home health care), and the balance between health services for the young versus the old. In other words, bioethics will grow from being a branch of applied philosophy to a meld of philosophy, economics, and policywonkism. A third safe prediction is that this debate will be unpleasant and unavoidable.

The Baby Boomers will force it upon us.

Artwork by Matt Wuerker. Copyright© 1998, Matt Wuerker. Distributed by Los Angeles Times Syndicate.

CHAPTER 6
HEALTH CARE 2020: POSSIBLE SCENARIOS

While writing *Health Care 2020*, we were struck by the thought that many people will view the likely changes in the U.S. health care system with a sense of unease. The health care system of the year 2020 will indeed take us into unfamiliar territory. As a result of the inevitable surge of aging Boomers, the way we finance and deliver public and private health care services will undergo dramatic changes in a few short years.

Just how short? Twenty-two years ago, a sweater-clad President Carter was about to address the nation in a fireside chat during which he would ask for mandatory temperature controls in buildings and for more car pooling. The world is running out of oil, the president would say—and few doubted his words. Yet today, even with Iraq's immense production of oil largely removed from the market, the inflation-adjusted price of gasoline at the pump is at an all-time low. The world is drowning in oil. In their assertion that we were running out of it, an American president's forecasters were dead wrong. The lesson is worth heeding: in two decades massive changes can occur in how we view public policy problems and how we go about resolving them.

While we offer here a host of creative solutions suggesting what impending public policy challenges are likely to be, we do not shy away from telling the bad news. The Ultimate Bad News is that we must cope with the health care demands of the immense and rapidly aging Baby Boomer generation.

This book describes a future American health care system radically different from the model in place in the late 1990s. We believe the following health care scenarios for the year 2020 range from barely possible but unlikely to very likely and perhaps inevitable.

Possible Outcomes

Scenario A

No sweat. Technology of some kind will either render medical care so cheap, or the economy so large, that providing medical and retirement comfort to the Boomer elderly will be a tolerable burden for the younger generations. The health care finance and delivery system can continue much "as is." The system of predominantly employment-based heath insurance will reach a smaller proportion of the population (see Chapter 2), but will remain largely intact. No major public policy changes are required. A generous Kidcare plan will be possible without undue strain on the public budget and will not unduly knock heads with the health care demands of the Baby Boomer elderly. These bounteous resources will put off any nasty bioethics questions of how to allocate scarce resources to senior citizens. No major changes in the health care delivery system are required.

This idyllic world would be a pleasant place in which to live. But we must be skeptical that it will happen.

Two possibilities exist. One is that medical technology will produce "magic bullets." Perhaps genetic engineering will have advanced so far by the year 2020 that preventing or treating defective DNA will cure so many maladies on an individual, onetime, basis that overall medical costs will fall dramatically. We do not discount that *possibility*, although the history of medical advances has generally been to drive costs *up*, not down. Some medical advances will allow us to treat currently treatable diseases more cheaply. Diseases presently treatable, but with poor prospects of a favorable patient outcome, may be routinely conquered. (The cheap Salk and Sabin polio vaccines made iron lungs unnecessary by eradicating the disease.)

Other advances raise costs by making currently untreatable conditions treatable. For example, new drug "cocktails" show results in controlling AIDS, but they are quite expensive. We have no doubt that health care in 2020 will be more *effective*. But it requires a huge leap of faith to assume that it will overall be *cheaper*.

There is also the question of the last six months or year of life, when over half of lifetime medical outlays occur. Unless one believes that medicine can produce immortality, that time will eventually come for all the Boomers. Medical advances will simply delay the time when those large expenditures will be made. And unless there is a societal bioethics consensus to "just let them die," those late-life medical expenditures *will* be made. We somehow doubt that the aged Boomers will form part of that consensus.

A second possibility is a Golden Age of Economic Growth as the result of an economy-wide productivity increase driven by the coming of age of

Information Technology (I.T.). Easy-to-use PCs, the Internet, and related technology based on ever cheaper and more efficient microchips propel productivity beyond anything in our historical experience, and grow the economic "pie" so rapidly that the best medical care and retirement income support are available to all Boomers at a relatively light cost to the young. The history of major innovations with economy-wide impact—railroads, chemicals, electricity, electronic broadcasting—is that they do increase productivity (output per worker). However, long-term economic projections already assume innovation. After all, if we all were to keep doing the same things in the same way, productivity growth would be zero. We look at history and observe that innovation in market economies always occurs. Therefore it will also occur in the future, and we already factor this into the projections of what the economy will do. For the Golden Age argument to work, Information Technology must be *quantitatively* different from all other past innovations. I.T. must drive productivity beyond levels outside our historical experience. I.T. must be vastly unlike anything we have ever seen before.

As with the medical care "magic bullet', we do not discount this *possibility*. The sky-high valuations given to Internet stocks and, to a lesser extent, other technology stocks, tell us that there are certainly market participants who believe this may happen. Adding "dot com" to a ticker symbol drives a stock up 25 percent.

Yet one must remain uneasy with the notion that I.T. will lead to high, perpetual-motion economic growth. No past innovation has repealed the business cycle. I.T. will not stop government from periodically making policy blunders which cause economic downturns. And it does no good to argue that I.T. is different because it has economy-wide implications. Did electricity have an impact on the entire economy? Did railroads?

An offshoot of the Golden Age argument is proposals advanced by President Clinton and others to shore up Medicare (and Social Security) by diverting the bulk of future federal budget surpluses to the Medicare (and Social Security) Trust Funds. These projected surpluses are the result of robust and sustained economic growth that began in the fourth quarter of 1992. They will, it is argued, delay by decades any tough choices about benefit and coverage levels, eligibility ages, etc.

This "solution" is superficially appealing and scores high political points. But it is vulnerable on a number of counts. Federal Reserve Chairman Alan Greenspan testified before Congress to exactly that on 28 January 1999.

First, and least, long-term projections of federal budget deficits or surpluses have been notoriously inaccurate. Federal forecasters from the executive branch of the Office of Management and Budget and the Congressional Budget Office have often been wrong by tens of billions of dollars over a *six-month* forecast. We don't really know what the federal budget surplus will be in 2001, 2005, or 2009, or even if there will be a surplus. This is counting the budgetary chickens before the economic egg has hatched.

More fundamentally, this solution displays no understanding of how future seniors' entitlements are really financed. As we stressed in Chapter 2, Medicare (and Social Security) in a given year come from current production in that year. One cannot put health care professionals and CAT scanners in a warehouse labeled "Medicare for the Baby Boomers in the year 2020." Putting a sizable chunk of future federal budget surpluses (if they materialize) into the Medicare (and Social Security) Trust Funds simply means that in a given year federal borrowing will be that much less than it otherwise would be because the revenue is not spent. It is an indirect way of paying down government debt which could be equally accomplished by buying back Treasury securities. The net effect of putting money into the Trust Funds is to reduce federal borrowing from external sources in a given year. Trust Fund assets still consist of government IOU's. The real question remains the size of the economic pie in the year 2020, not the amount of paper promises to pay in the Trust Funds. Reducing government borrowing is a good thing in that it increases the pool of national savings available for investment and therefore tends to increase the rate of economic growth. But most econometric studies put the increased growth rate on the order of tenths of percentage points a year.

This is hardly a Golden Age kind of number.

Overall, we must rate the probability of a Scenario A-type outcome as low. We hope we are wrong. If Scenario A comes to pass, then a major premise of this book—that Baby Boomer demographics will force drastic changes in how we finance health care and take care of the elderly in general—is also wrong. That would be fine with us. The sometimes unpleasant choices we have outlined will not have to be made.

But for the reasons we have outlined, we would not put many chips on Scenario A.

Scenario B

Intergenerational Warfare. The worst case scenario. No Scenario A "magic bullet" is in the cards, but we try to maintain current seniors' entitlements at their current level of generosity.

Scenario B is by no means farfetched. Boomers may adopt an attitude of "I have paid taxes for Social Security and Medicare for most of my life, and now I want mine. Any politician who suggests benefit cuts or retirement age increases will learn at the polls that this course is a serious mistake.

There are 76 million of us to enforce that threat—and most of us vote."

Scenario B grows more likely each year the political classes delay educating the public about the true financial future of their retirement and health care entitlements. Boomers are entitled to some decent period of time to make more provisions for their own future retirement and health care. Washington cannot march up to the cliff of the year 2011 and say "Whoops!! Those promises we made...well...." Boomers would then have more than adequate reason to rebel.

Yet, while we have noted that discussions about changes in Medicare and Social Security are not quite the political death wish they once were, there remains a reluctance to advance any but painless solutions ("devote the coming budget surplus to save Social Security and bolster Medicare"). Tough political choices require both a crisis and a consensus. The problem is that, when the crisis is obvious to all, the search for a consensus may be too late.

Such a world would be most unappealing. The young would face total marginal tax rates approaching 50 percent or more by the year 2020. And these rates would only increase as the next decade unfolds. Economic growth would stagnate. The young would feel a sense of understandable hostility toward their parents and grandparents. At the same time, fewer of the young would be covered by employment-based health insurance (see Chapter 2). Many of the young would either go uninsured or buy individual or family policies, from shrunken after-tax incomes, while trying to purchase a home and educate their children. Ways and means will be hard, perhaps impossible, to balance.

Scenario B should be thought of as the Greedy Geezer syndrome. The Boomers retain Medicare at age 65, supplemented by relatively cheap "Medigap" policies. Their health care finance is rock solid.

The health care finance of the young is much more doubtful. There are two likely outcomes of Scenario B. One is that the young will take a much more active interest in the bioethics debate. If the seniors' entitlement burden is unbearable, they may well ask just when an old person has a "duty to die." A second is a likely interest in some form of national health insurance (which we do not favor). The young may be tempted to reason, "I'm paying for all this medical care for the old through government programs. Why can't the government give me some, too?" While this reasoning may be fallacious, it could well gain currency. Indeed, we are persuaded that the most likely route to a nationalized health care system lies in an attempt to maintain Medicare and Social Security "as is" until the Baby Boomers drop their retirement bomb on society.

We would like to think that the Boomers will not want to impoverish their children. But one cannot be entirely confident about this. The Boomers *will* have paid in a great deal of money to support their parents' entitlements. And they *will* be reluctant to give up part of their promised benefits, particularly if that decision is delayed until retirement looms. Then there is the Boomer culture itself. As we explained in Chapter 1, the Boomers have always had their way, and they sense this. By virtue of their numbers, they tend to control. They are the "Me" generation. Perhaps they will put "me" first one more time.

Overall, Scenario B is unlikely (perhaps because we just don't want to believe it). But the Scenario B "disaster" is at least as likely as the Scenario A "magic bullet." Children and parents at each others throats is not a future we relish.

Scenario C

Both private and public health care finance are radically changed. Painless solutions are not forthcoming (Scenario A), but neither does the Boomer health care demand cause societal upheaval (Scenario B). Employment-based insurance essentially ends. Medicare is scaled back but does not disappear, and cost increases are held somewhat in check by introducing more competition in bidding and purchasing. Medical Savings Accounts become common among the general population.

Our vision of Health Care 2020 is Scenario C. It is by far the most likely. Scenario C has these elements:

1) The political leadership finally bestirs itself to change the rules of the game on seniors' entitlements well before the first Boomers are close to what they perceive as retirement. Eligibility ages are raised and/or benefits are cut and/or taxes are raised to fund seniors' entitlements, including Medicare. Benefit cuts and/or retirement age increases are not so steep as to incur open rebellion among Boomers. Their Baby Buster children will eventually pay higher tax rates to support them, but not so much higher that intergenerational warfare breaks out. No one is happy, but no one is scorchingly mad.

Whichever political party is perceived to have engineered this imperfect compromise will incur the wrath of both the Boomers and the Baby Busters. Boomers eventually will not get all of what they think they have been promised. Busters eventually will pay more. For the United States to avoid a Scenario B disaster, these changes should occur by the middle of the next decade. Perhaps both parties should have political consultants contriving how to *lose* the Year 2000 elections. Blame the other guy for the goring of sacred entitlement cows. In reality, neither party will be willing to shoulder the entire blame for major changes in seniors' entitlements. The blame must be spread around for any change to be politically viable.

That's why the magic word is "bipartisan." We had a National *Bipartisan* Commission on the Future of Medicare debating whether to shift Medicare to a "premium support" system. Premium support would subsidize the elderly to enroll in a health plan and would be a radical departure from the current system, which pays medical bills directly. The hope is that competition might reduce the rate of increase in medical costs.

2) The tax exclusion for employment-based health insurance will be repealed as part of this deal. It will be replaced by a general tax credit for purchase of individual health insurance. The tax exclusion never made much sense except as a way to get around World War II wage controls. Boomers will support it as getting something in the way of retirement health insurance when Medicare no longer is so generous. Business will support the repeal and replacement as a means of taking the pressure off them to be the primary suppliers of retirement health insurance for their former employees. Both the Left and Right have ideological reasons to want repeal. And the young, faced with no better alternative, should acquiesce.

3) What of this Brave New World of no tax benefit to employees of employment-based health insurance?

First, Medical Savings Accounts will be an attractive option for many. MSAs combine a high-deductible health insurance policy (usually $2,000-$4,000) with a savings account (usually $1,000-$2,000). Annual, smaller, medical expenses are paid from the savings account. If unusually large medical expenses are incurred, the high-deductible policy kicks in and pays all expenses over the deductible amount. In any given year, the individual's maximum exposure to medical expenses is the difference between the savings account and the deductible amount. At the end of the year, any unspent amount in the savings account may be kept by the individual.

Individuals could use the health insurance credit to purchase a high-deductible insurance policy. Repeal of the health insurance tax exclusion for employment-based insurance would increase federal revenue by about $100 billion, enough to fund the purchase of a high-deductible health insurance policy for most Americans if passed back as a health insurance tax credit. If the law is changed to allow further tax-deductible contributions to an MSA, MSAs will become the health care financing standard of the year 2020.

This last course by itself solves many of today's problems. Health care costs are driven by the third-party nature of payment. Someone else—the employer's insurance carrier or the government—pays our bills. Many health care services can be shopped around. We don't shop around because that spending is "not our money." Under MSAs, we spend "our" money (which one can keep if not spent) on small medical bills, and the insurance company high-deductible policy pays for the big bills. There is an incentive to ask about price and get a bid from another provider.

4) Medical care for poorer Americans—both old and young—will be financed and delivered in new ways. Consider those Boomers who, for whatever

reason, have not made adequate provision to prepare for their retirement health care needs.

Boomers of all incomes are currently happy with Medicare. Medicare relieves them of primary responsibility for the medical costs of their parents. Medicaid finances nursing home care in many cases and relieves the Boomer child of the responsibility for caring for the parent at home. But as we describe in this book, the massive numbers of Boomers will upset this apple cart.

Since neither author is a practicing politician, we can touch the "third rails" of seniors' entitlements and live another day. We confidently predict that retirement programs such as Medicare will not be nearly so generous to the Boomer oldsters of the next century. Through a combination of benefit cuts or eligibility age increases, late 1990s Medicare will be transformed early in the next century.

Does this mean we expect to see hordes of destitute Boomers unable to access health care services of any sort? Of course not.

First, if (as we expect) the employment-based health insurance tax exclusion is repealed and replaced by a universal credit for health insurance purchases, every American, including the graying Boomers, will have access to a high-deductible health insurance policy. Second, Medicare may be less generous, but it is not going to fade away entirely. Medicare may well be transformed from what it is today into funding the savings account portion of MSAs for seniors (perhaps with a temporary way station of premium support).

For the nonelderly, there are losers. But not all of the nonelderly. Among the young, those who would have otherwise have been without health insurance will now have high-deductible health insurance financed through a tax credit. They "win." We argue it is not possible to maintain all seniors' entitlements, and the elderly Boomers likely will retain health care through a combination of a tax credit for high-deductible insurance and some contribution from whatever is left of Medicare. Someone will pay a price. There is no bottomless cornucopia guaranteeing health care without pain to everyone in the graying Boomer era.

Those someones who will pay the price are the young who would otherwise be covered under an employment-based system. They trade their current tax exclusion for all employment-based health insurance for a high-deductible "catastrophic" policy. They are "worse off." They have lost their low- or no-deductible policies for something which requires them to pay for the first physician visit when Junior or Junioretta feels bad.

Yet not is all lost for even these folks. We argue in Chapter 2 that business will be a part of the coalition to repeal the tax exclusion, but many business firms (relieved that they will not have to be the primary supplier of retirement health insurance) will voluntarily stay in the health business. Business firms may contribute to the "savings account" portion of MSAs. Or, as is highly likely, new insurance products will spring forth. Insurance companies will find a ready market for low- or zero-deductible policies up to a low level of expenditures, a sort of insurance variety of the savings account portion of MSAs. Business firms may well wish to contribute toward the purchase of these new insurance vehicles because of the still lingering feeling among employees that "my employer pays for my health insurance."

Granted, business involvement with employment-based health insurance will now be with after-tax dollars to the employee. A rational employee should not care whether he or she gets more cash or some kind of health insurance support from the employer when the tax preference for health insurance is repealed. But old habits die hard.

At the same time, state and federal leaders will not be idle. They will look for innovative ways to spread limited health care dollars. They will find those innovative policies, perhaps even some we suggest in this book. Properly designed home health care programs might be one strategy.

By the year 2020, the nonelderly will also benefit from the Boomer-driven burst of health care innovation. Carving new MSAs from Medicaid to empower even the poorest Americans with patient choice is one strong possibility. Or perhaps expanded access to the Earned Income Tax Credit as a source for medical care funds to help low-income people get health care services will become a reality.

Children from low-income families will see changes in the way they access health care services. Federal Kidcare legislation from the late 1990s is spawning efforts in statehouses across the nation to extend heath care insurance to the children of families too "rich" for Medicaid.

No one is comfortable seeing children of the working poor without health insurance (not the same thing as being without access to health care). But, as we describe in Chapters 2 and 3, the Boomers' exit from the workforce, and the subsequent decline in employment-based insurance, will send parents searching for whatever supplements they can find for the high-deductible policies we envision when the health insurance income tax exclusion is eventually repealed.

There are dangers here. Otherwise uninsured families will look at their slightly poorer brethren and note that they are receiving Kidcare assistance from the government. These lower-middle-class families may become highly vocal advocates for government help for them also. Where is the "firewall" where this stops?

Kidcare could well follow the footsteps of Medicare by the year 2020. Kidcare HMOs could arise, attempting to control costs through reducing physician payments, limiting parents' choice of providers, and cutting services.

More kids might be receiving basic services, but Kidcare bureaucrats, rather than doctors in consultation with parents, will hold the whip hand.

This also is not a prospect we relish.

Conclusion

In describing the probable American health care system of the year 2020, we are reminded of James Hagerty, Dwight Eisenhower's presidential press secretary. Christopher Matthews writes that Hagerty at times was left with the unenviable task of presenting to the American people information that many would find unsettling. Hagerty recounts, "Eisenhower would say, 'Do it this way.' And I would say, 'If I go to the press conference and say what you want me to say, I would get hell.' With that, he would smile, get up and walk around the desk, pat me on the back and say, 'My boy, better you than me'."

Health Care 2020 is not a doom-and-gloom book. The Baby Boomers will cause a serious rethinking of what most of us have come to think of as the natural state of affairs. Employment-based insurance will shrink and the tax exclusion which drives it will be repealed. Medical Savings Accounts will be prevalent. Seniors' entitlements will be reneged upon. The possibility of war among the Baby Boomers and Baby Busters is quite real, although we think that will not happen. And the Busters will wind up with a raw deal, but not one with which they cannot live.

The health care debate over the next twenty-one years will be uncomfortable for many even if the eventual outcome is a livable one. We will have to rethink our paradigms. We can do it.

Welcome to health care in the year 2020. Better we write about it now than for you to learn about it too late.

INDEX

0578   72